CAT CREEK TALES

STORIES FROM AN (ALMOST) FORGOTTEN PAST

BY

ADREN McLANE

ISBN: 978-1-7341437-3-7

Printed in the United States of America

Burnt Sage Publications paperback/October 2022

Cover Design: Gary Randall

Dedication

To grandfathers everywhere

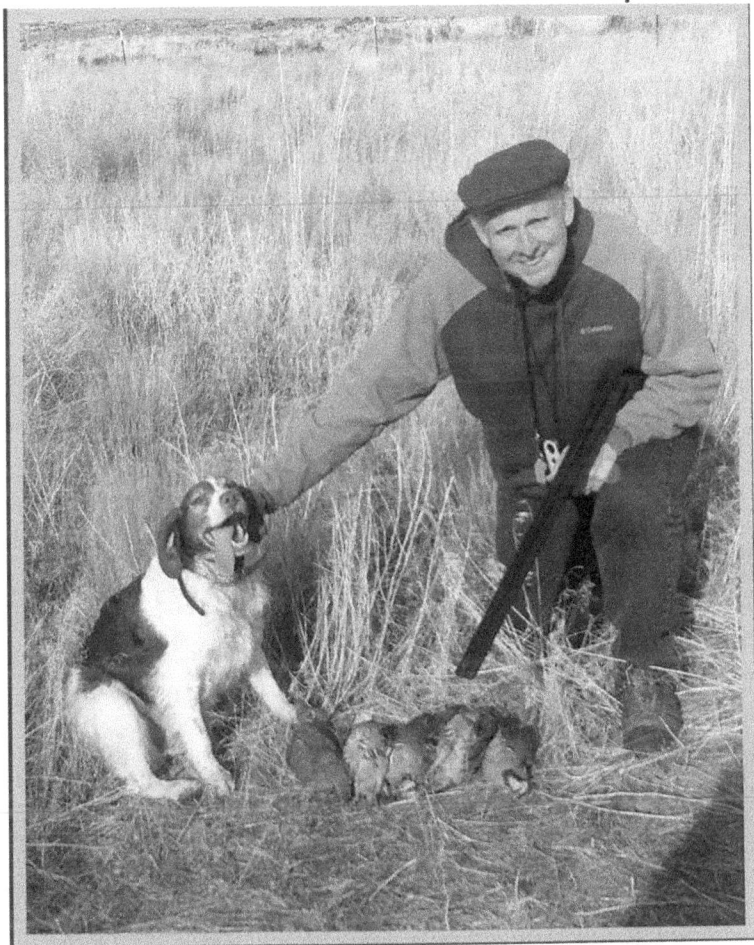

CAT CREEK

As creeks go Cat Creek really wasn't all that big. A fella could jump across it in most places, even one as small as I was when I grew up there. What it did have were a few spots where shell crackers would hole up and we would go down to fish out of a couple of those holes, hook a dozen or so and take them home for Mama to cook. By we, I mean my brother Mel and me. We kind of hung together because there weren't a lot of other kids to play with close by. Neighbors were farmers just like we were, no one living particularly close to each other.

I was probably six when the first girl who was around my age ever showed up at our place. She wanted to go fishing with us. At first we were greatly annoyed at the idea of a GIRL wanting to butt in on our MAN time, especially since school was starting the next week and we only had so much freedom left before the State of Georgia said we had to go back to Cat Creek State Prison...or school as Mama called it. We agreed to let her come along but only if she did what we told her to do. On the way down to the creek we'd decided this was our secret fishing hole that must NEVER be discovered by outsiders, especially a girl. So we told her she had to wear a blindfold. It was the only way we'd let her join us. Well, she hollered and hollered about that idea but finally agreed...dumb girl. We'd never expected anyone to be that gullible.

Mel had an old dirty rag he used for just about everything and since it was the only thing we had near to being a blindfold, we tied it over her eyes and led her on down to the creek. We managed to keep her from tripping over all the stumps, pine cones, and other lethal things on the ground and finally got her far enough into the woods so's we could fish one of the holes. When we took the blindfold off she hollered about it stinking so bad that she had to breath out of her mouth. I made some smart comment about not knowing how she could breath when all she seemed able to do was holler. Well that set her off again and Mel and I just shrugged our shoulders and got to digging for worms.

Best bait in the world for almost any fish is a good juicy worm. Most especially since all we had for hooks were some old safety pins we managed to get from Mama. I'll tell you, they worked great for catching a fish so long as you never give him slack. Since the hook was barbless that fish was gone the second he got a slack line. I hear tell there's now a bunch of states outlawing barbed hooks altogether. From what I understand they's regulatin' trying to preserve the species. Well, dang it. If that's the case, then why the heck do they allow anyone to fish at all? I kept thinking about that and wonderin' what a fish mighta been thinking when he got hooked "Oh, I'm okay, there's no barb".

Emily was her name now that I think about it. Emily Hartwing. What a name. When we first started digging, she asked us what we were doing and why were we playing in the dirt and not fishing. Mel and I just looked at her as if she had suddenly admitted to being from Mars. The more she asked the more certain we grew that she just might be. Anyway, we laughed at her and explained you gotta have bait to catch fish and this is were the bait lives.

We got the worms dug up and headed over to the hole…one of our best ones. Now when I say fishin' hole I ain't talking about a real hole like in the ground. It was only a wider spot in the creek with about five or six feet of water instead of one foot deep like most of the creek was.

It hadn't rained in about three weeks so there hadn't been much mud washed down from the farms and that deep water was almost clear. We could actually see a couple of fish when we got there. We saw 'em scurry off under some roots of an old cypress tree on the other bank. We unwound our line off the poles and grabbed some worms out of the can then handed the can to Emily. We thought she had done gone crazy 'cause she started hollerin' and makin' kind of a funny squeaking sound. After a couple of minutes o' starin' at her we finally figured out she was not a friend of worms.

Mel was all for taking her back to the house but I said I wasn't gonna walk all the way back to the house and back to the fishin' hole just because some dumb girl was scared of a toothless blind worm. I'd just bait her hook for her and that would be the end of it. I found out in short order that this process was only good for one fish.

I stuck that worm on the hook and quick as a flea can jump, she slapped that water with the pole so hard they probably had a tidal wave over in China the next week. Needless to say, it didn't help inspire complacency in the fish in that pool either. But, as luck would have it, the waves calmed down and the fish decided it wasn't some ol' skunk ape taking a bath and grabbing for 'em. One of 'em darted out and seized that worm and the hook seized him. I'm telling you he must have been an old grandpappy, 'cause he took hold of that hook and he started a swimming around like one of those baracuddies I'd read about. Emily took to hollerin' and we were screamin' at her to flip him out on the ground. I guess we won the hollerin' contest 'cause about then she yanked on that pole and the fish, line, and pole all landed about 20 feet behind us.

We all ran over to the fish and were telling Emily about how good a job she'd done and now she had to grab the fish and put him on the stringer. Well sir, I reckon that was the last straw as far as she was concerned because she said no lady would EVER touch a dead fish and certainly not a live one and she turned to stomp off home. Only thing was she'd been blindfolded so had no idea as to which way was home. First she headed upstream through the woods but we knew that only took you further into the swamp and we told her she was going the wrong way. She came back and started heading downstream and we hollered at her again that she was heading deeper into the swamp and she was like to get eaten by an old gator if she went there… if she didn't get bit by a nasty cottonmouth. That finally done her in and she came back and plopped down on an old oak log.

I started to tell her she best not be sittin' on that particular log but the bees beat me to it and told her for me. She must have jumped five feet in the air, screamed like a screech owl and headed for that pool we were expecting to get our supper out of. We were, of course, rolling on the ground laughing by the time she hit the water. Only thing was we couldn't laugh for long because bees, being of a democratic mind about things, took after us too. Like it or not that pool was the only bit of water in range for us to jump into and there we were, Mel, Emily, and I and not a one of us was laughing.

We had to stay under water and keep dunking our heads down so's not to get stung. After about 20 minutes the bees figured we'd got their message. When we finally climbed out of the water we remembered that poor old perch still lying on the ground with a hook in his mouth. I was kind of put out at that. We'd pretty much figgered that being soaked clean through put an end to our fishing for the day and all we had to show for our work was one fish. Granted he was a biggun but not near big enough for us to take him home. I surely hated to see him just dead and wasted because of a girl.

I went over and picked him up. He wasn't doing that mouthin' thing you see fish do when they's out of water but he was still a wiggling, so I took out the hook and tossed him back in that pool. Danged if he didn't flip around a couple of times and head to the cypress roots. We wrapped the lines on the poles and told Emily we weren't gonna blindfold her on the way out cause she was such a bother coming in. Besides, I kind of figured she wasn't going to be bothering us about going fishing again.

So with that, we buried the remaining worms and headed on home; wet, mad, and covered with little bumps from that danged bunch of democratic bees. What was worse, Papa threatened to give us a few more bumps when we showed up lookin' like that. Emily's daddy made the same threat and in those days there weren't no such ideas as child abuse. If you got into trouble at school or somewhere, like as not you got a whipping at school and had another one waiting for you when you got home. Bees weren't the only things being democratic in those days.

The curious thing was that about a week later, Mel and I managed to sneak off and head back down to that hole and see if we couldn't get that big old fish, and some of his kinfolk too, but we never got a bite from that hole for the rest of that summer. I always figgered that big fella we caught had a long conversation with his folks down in that hole. Worms were off their diets from then on! All I know is that particular hole never did offer up any good results after that day.

My thoughts were pretty firm when it came to the idea of having any women along for fishing ever again and I sure didn't let another one get a chance to talk me into bringing her along. That included my wife many years later. Ethylene loved to eat and cook fish but not long after we were married she told me it was my job to go to the meat market and hers to fix what I brought home…especially if the meat market involved anything with a boat, shotgun, or rifle. She appreciated the product but had no designs on being involved in the process. This worked fine for me at that time and probably helped save our marriage on a number of occasions. She was a fine cook and I think probably could have made a rock taste good if needs be. Sometimes I reckon marrying that gal was about the only right thing I ever did in my life.

But that's a story for another day. I may tell it someday but folks'd have to promise me not to repeat it or I'd pay the dickens for telling it.

HURRICANES
(WHAT NOT TO TELL)

In 18 and 98 I was just shy of turning three and can only remember some of what happened the day the big 'cane hit the coast down south of Savannah. My recollections of exactly what took place are not as precise now as they were a couple years later when we got caught in one that had mostly died out by the time it got to us. She'd come ashore down on the northwest corner of Florida near Pensacola and wandered on over to us a day or so later. It didn't do as much wind damage but it sure did drop a bucket or two of water.

Back in those days folks didn't have much time to get out of the way of those big blows and it was only the day before the storm hit that folks had any idea a 'cane might be heading our way. There are many old wives' tales (the tales are old, not the wives) about "reading the signs" on approaching storms. I figured I never was much good at reading as I've been caught many a time out in the woods when a cold front moved through or a thunderstorm burst the sky with hail and all. I don't so much mind getting rained on if I'm at least somewhat prepared but I remember one afternoon...well, I'll mention that some later.

Back to the 'cane of '98. At the time I was just a tad taller than a grasshopper, if you reckon it was a small one, so pretty much everything looked giant to me. We had an old oak tree near the house that was probably just a baby when General Washington was stompin' around cussing at King George. Least ways, that's how Papa described it. Mama shushed him about referring to cussing, which kind of amused us as we'd heard Papa, more'n a time or two, "talking" to that pair of mules we had one summer--and only just one summer.

That old oak tree was nigh on to 40 feet high and seemed to be just as wide. It had a couple of branches that hung over one end of the house and while the big kids, I mean my brothers and cousins, risked life or limb getting out onto those branches, I could do it easy being as I was so small. Even though I was only three, or near 'bouts, I was already a middlin' climber. I reckon Mama would o' had a fit if she'd ever caught me up there.

The day before that 'cane hit us Mama was fussing that the chickens had quit laying. Then, long about mid-morning, a whole passel of seagulls flew over. "They's heading away from the coast," she cautioned. "You all stay close now 'cause there's a storm acoming." And that was about all she said.

But the sun was shining with nary a cloud in the sky and it was shaping up to be a hot day, already near 90 on that old tin thermometer hangin' on the barn wall, so we young'uns were sure confused. Not Papa though. He'd learned to pay attention to Mama, and her Mama and his, too, I reckon. He didn't question things they were saying regarding the weather.

He went out and dispatched a couple of old roosters that were always fighting, and directed us boys in cleaning up loose things around the yard. That only took about five minutes because neither parent was of a mind to let anything clutter the yard...or the house for that matter. Mama said a messy house was a sign of messy mind and the Lord didn't like neither and to mind how we left things laying around.

It wasn't till after that storm had come and gone that she explained a bit on how she knew. She was right of course and the funny thing I remember her saying afterwards was she knew it was coming but she hadn't reckoned on just how bad it was going to be.

In those days storms didn't have names. A storm was just the first, second, or third one (or more) of a particular year. It was 'most a lifetime later (hers) that the government decided to give a storm a name and then they started giving 'em women's names. That sure wrinkled a few skirts for a time. There was a storm in 19 and 35 down in Key West that they just called The Great Storm but I reckon if they'd had female names at the time they'd o' called it Eleanore after FDR's wife cause o' the rumors folks down here had heard about her. I reckon they weren't very polite so I'll just leave that for folks to chew on a bit.

Late in the afternoon the wind got real calm and it turned so muggy even the water was sweatin'. I was in the back yard playing marbles with the cat--anything to keep from having to move around very much. Even the cat mostly just laid there aswitching her tail. Long about dark Mama called us in for a cold supper. Mama said it was too hot for cooking so we could do with some leftover chicken and whatever else she could find in the ice box that didn't need heating; said it was going to be a bad night and we didn't need a hot stove to add to any misery that might befall us. Well, I do remember being kind of scared about that and that was even before Papa said we needed to sleep in our daytime clothes in case things got bad and we had to go off somewhere for safety. That made my siblings mighty nervous 'cause they knew Savannah wasn't exactly the Rocky Mountains. A high place in Savannah wouldn't be much over 40 or 50 feet above sea level. We didn't exactly live in Savannah itself but in a little town about 20 mile or so west o' there. Turns out, that's probably what helped us in the end.

Mama shooed us to bed long about eight or so and told us to just be quiet and get to sleep and, no matter what, even if the wind picked up, we was to stay inside the house. Well, being told what to do and doing just that are oft times mutually exclusive to a boy but like all the rest I went to bed and, ain't no surprise to most folks, I was asleep pretty quick…leastwise for a while. Only thing was, near on to the middle of the night that storm started whipping up and the wind and rain was something amazing to hear. Not being aware that I might be in any kind of danger, I looked out the window and when the lightening flashed I could see that old oak tree a whipping around like it was dancing. All 'ceptin for those two branches by the house.

I'd heard a story a few days before about something called a parachute and it was a big old umbrella like thing that folks would strap on and jump off of cliffs or out of a balloon and just float on down to the ground like a leaf. That got me to thinking about a big ol' umbrella Papa had given Mama some time back. I snuck out of bed and grabbed that umbrella from behind the front door, opened the door a crack and squeezed out. I scampered around the side of the house and to this day I can't recall just how I managed to hang on to that umbrella, big as it was, and climb up that oak tree on to the roof of the house. But I did. The house wasn't but a single story and that probably saved my life, my being ignorant of the laws of gravity. I figured I'd just float on down and land softly on the ground. I remember waiting a bit for a big gust. When it came I opened the umbrella and gripped it with both hands. I didn't have to jump. The wind grabbed it and we both went off that roof faster than I could tell this sentence.

Well, I learned a couple valuable lessons that night. I reckon I probably learned more than a couple but the two things I recall best are; one, umbrella's ain't parachutes and, two, you have to obey the law of gravity. I got blowed about 10 feet away from the house but I didn't float. I went to the ground like it was a pulling on me hard and while I didn't break anything, I sure didn't do that umbrella any good. It was in such a sorry state all I could think to do was get rid of it as fast as I could and get back to bed 'fore I was missed. I can't recall how I did either one. I do remember being pretty darned sore for a couple of days but not so anyone ever caught on. I looked at my rump in the mirror the next day and if I'd have been caught that night, my rear wouldn't have looked any more bruised than it did from full contact with the ground. Fred guessed what had happened when he caught me in the bathroom and saw my bruises. He must have figured I had been punished enough 'cause he never told.

I remember looking at that oak tree the next day. It looked like a chicken plucked off her feathers but it was still standing. As far as I know, it's still standing today. I guess it goes to show, like everything else, when you've got good roots, you can survive a lot of bad things.

Years later when we were all sitting around recollecting on things I learned more about that storm and about how much damage it had done, especially down in Savannah. Seems it killed a lot of folks and quite a few animals. I heard tell over a thousand chickens just disappeared from a chicken farm a few miles away and there were even some folks who vanished as well.

I didn't tell Mama what I'd done 'til I got back from France and I reckon I shouldn't have mentioned it then. It was one of the few times in my life I got slapped. She didn't hit me hard 'cause she was laughing—she'd always blamed Papa for using that umbrella and not bringing it back. And she was thankful and relieved to have me back home.

Like I said earlier, I don't mind being caught in a storm if I'm prepared. When I was long about 16 I was out bird hunting when a danged impressive thunderstorm blew in. I had Stony with me at the time and I knew there was no way I'd make it back to the horse I'd tied over by the creek, much less make it home. I found an old oak tree, grabbed Stony, and clung to him underneath that tree. That storm blew in hard and fast. Lightning bolts were ashootin' high, wide, and lethal. I hadn't yet learned about not being under a tree during a storm like that and I reckon I was lucky that day as nothing more serious than wet happened to either of us. One bolt hit so close to us I could have sworn Saint Peter was whispering to get ready for check-in. Then it was gone as quick as it had popped up.

I wiped Stony down a bit and he was rearing to go back to the hunt. Seems nothing ever really bothered that dog. I figured he must have thought all that thunder was somebody shooting at birds--big birds he couldn't see. We wandered on back to the horse and I learned then what happens in a thunderstorm. That horse was in the creek as dead as a rock. Seems lightening likes water and if you figure on it, a horse ain't nothing but a whole lot of water. I guess it was a stroke of luck I hadn't jumped on him to try to get back to the house before the storm hit.

Up until that time I'd not been afraid of lightning but even though lots of years have passed, I still get uncomfortable when the rumbling starts. When old Thor starts throwing those bolts around I make sure I'm inside somewhere--anywhere.

I think about that old oak tree now and then. I remind myself to consider the consequences when planning on doing something that sounds like "fun". And I figure, like that old oak I, too, have pretty good roots anchored deep with the Good Lord and I try to not worry too much about something I can't control.

HORSELESS CARRIAGES

We'd heard about horseless carriages of course but being so far out of the big city we just didn't see 'em very often. We couldn't just sit and wait for a car to go by in those early days. I remember my little brother Mel one time reckoned they were such a big deal it took three people to enjoy the news; one to see it, one to hear it, and a third to run and tell folks. In those days we called them automobiles. I can't remember when people started just calling them cars. Everything's different nowadays.

We weren't off in the woods necessarily. We lived just south of the road that went from Hahira to Lakeland but the BIG city was Valdosta. I had a couple of sisters who had married pharmacists. They both set up pharmacies down there and we'd go visit 'em every couple of months or so. Since I was the oldest boy, and Mel the youngest, the two of us would go down and spend a couple of weeks with them during the summer. We liked that. Corrine and her husband lived on a little lake that held a passel of fish. Mel and I were more'n glad to help reduce the overcrowding.

I was born in Savannah and spent my first few years there but I really grew up on a farm north of Valdosta in Georgia. Valdosta is 20 miles or so north of the Florida - Georgia state line. When I was a boy there were about 5600 folks living there. When you consider Hahira had only about 260, Valdosta seemed like a pretty big city. Lumber was the business that helped build Valdosta and there is a lumber mill there still as well as a paper mill, which you can keep. The smell from one of those places is just something I never could abide.

One thing I remember about going to Valdosta is that Mel and I used to wander on down to the old courthouse square and listen to the old Confederate soldiers. They'd sit on the benches telling stories about the war. (That was the War Between the States. At that time we hadn't had a serious war since that one.) Those old timers sure could make a kid wonder at all they had seen and been a part of. They'd run us off if they caught us listenin' 'cause they didn't use language you'd likely hear on a Sunday morning. War must have been pretty bad, 'cause once in a while I'd hear a couple of 'em kind of get going on some battle or something and then stop all of a sudden. Then they'd just hug for a bit then head on home. I learned a few years later there wasn't nothing wrong with that and I could sure understand why a soldier was that way. Remembering those conversations helped me several years later to understand some of the things old Uncle Sam made me do and how to deal with those events.

Both of my granddaddies were in that war. Grandpa Smith died a'fore I was born, but Grandpa Williams survived it but he didn't talk much about it, least ways not if he thought we were anywhere in hearing distance. He had several brothers and they all served the South and he'd lost two in the fighting. He'd owned slaves before the war. When I was still a young'n there was an old colored couple living in a little house back of ours. They'd been slaves and after the war they didn't have no where to go so they just stayed on with the family. Grandpa paid 'em to help with the farming and housework.

They'd been married for nigh on to 50 years but never had children… none that lived. They were always 'specially nice to us little'ns. Uncle Zeb, as we called him, made some of the best darned cane syrup you ever tasted. His name was Zebullon Franklin Williams. He had picked out his full name when they were emancipated and he chose Franklin as his middle name for Ben Franklin and ours for their last name. His wife was Millicent Abigail Williams. She said she picked Abigail because that was the wife of John Adams who had always been a strong anti-slavery advocate.

Now before folks get riled up about my using the term colored, you have to remember that's what they called each other and that was the language we all used. No disrespect was ever intended in any manner.

I remember sitting out on their little porch one evening. I asked them how come they stayed on and were they bitter about being slaves. Uncle Zeb said he weren't exactly bitter but only sad and figger'd it was gonna take a long time to get the hate put away for a lot o' folks, both colored and white. He said there weren't no point in hating and that the best thing to do was ask the Lord for forgiveness for all the pain and suffering that had occurred. He said they stayed on with Granddaddy Williams and then my daddy after because my family had always treated them kindly, even though 45 years before this they were considered property and, like I said, they didn't have no place else to go. Traveling for a colored person was not an easy thing even if you had money but being colored and broke surely reduced your chances of re-locatin'.

I'm sure my daddy would have whipped me for asking personal questions like that but I was only 6 or 7 at the time and didn't think about that. When old Zeb died in 19 and 12, it hit us all pretty hard. Darned thing is, he died the same day that ship sank…the Titanic. Mama said it was fitting for him to go that day 'cause he was a Titanic of a man in many ways. Miss Millicent stayed on with us for another six years before she joined Uncle Zeb. I remember wondering at the time if the Titanic had gone down so they'd have a nice boat to ride across the river Jordan. Kind of makes you wonder.

I was in France fighting the Kaiser when I got a letter from Mama telling me about Miss Millicent. I sat down in that trench and cried a bit and then smiled remembering Miss Milly's cooking and how I missed it and realized I was gonna miss it for good now. She was a good soul and I realized sitting in that trench that it didn't matter what color you were on the outside, it's what color you were inside that really mattered. Mama had said in the letter that they had laid Miss Millicent next to Uncle Zeb in the family cemetery down the road and had put the graves up closer to the family 'stead of over in the corner where the slaves had been buried prior. There were no objections. As far as we were concerned, they were family.

I see I strayed off my remembering a lot further than I intended.

That first car that came along in 1907 was an Oldsmobile if I remember correct. The thing came a tearing down the road and must have been doing 25 per. There was a stop sign at the intersection of the Hahira road and Cat Creek road…right in front of our house. He managed to stop but not before bouncing almost completely out of that rig. He'd hit a couple of big old ruts that crossed the road and was cussing a blue streak when he finally did get stopped. Papa walked on out to him and told him to stop hollering and swearing or by God, he'd yank him out of that rig and split his britches with a belt. That young feller couldn't have been more than 16 or 17 years old and, unlike me, Papa was a pretty big man…6'3" and well over 200 pounds. Being a farmer, he wasn't exactly a weakling.

Well, the fella calmed down fast at that. He did manage to finally ask who put those ruts across the road. Papa just smiled and said nobody.

Well, it wasn't exactly nobody but in a way that was kind of true. Those ruts were caused when we skidded two big ol' pine logs across the road for a new barn. It was raining like it does there some times and the ground was pretty soft. We'd all been involved in helping get the bark off those trees and had forgot about the ruts. We'd never considered them of particular importance. A horse would just step over them and a farm buggy was slow and hardy. I reckon the funniest part of that whole event was Papa. He was so annoyed about that fella teaching us some new words he never did fill in those ruts. The county finally did so about 3 years later. And I had moved on long before they paved that road many years after that.

Seems like folks are getting in more and more of a hurry these days so the government puts in speed bumps. They don't seem to get them to just relax a bit and slow down. Every time I go over one of those danged speed bumps, I remember that first car and that fella and I forget all about being annoyed at them and just kind o' smile inside.

Papa thought that fella taught us some new words but we'd heard 'em all when Papa caught a coon with a mouthful of chicken running out of the hen coop one morning. He was a pious man but I reckon he could've held his own in a saloon if he had been a drinking man and there'd been a saloon nearby...but he wasn't and there wasn't.

THE NIGHT THE HA'NTS STOLE
THE MOON CAKE

My Mama's mother was a Smith. She passed away before I was born so it seems most of my childhood was spent amongst the Williams clan whatever the occasion and no matter the time of year. Grandma Williams was my father's mother. Papa called her Myma and I reckon that was a pretty good name 'cause we all took to addressing her so. She must have not minded 'cause I disrecollect ever calling her by any other name.

The year was 1910 and I was fixen' to start school. I started in pestering Mama about when Grandma Williams was coming to visit. She'd been down to see us earlier in the year but I still looked forward to her coming 'cause she'd bake cookies—all kinds of cookies—and candy. And I surely had my mouth watering for treats in my lunch box. Once in a while, maybe when she was tired of all those cookies, she'd bake what she called The Moon cake. It wasn't nothing but a round chocolate cake with white frosting on it but she said it looked like a full moon. It did, at that, so the name stuck and we all called it Myma's Moon cake.

Mama said Myma wasn't coming down until Thanksgiving and for a 6 year-old boy that was at least a century away. So I had to commit to serving my time at the Lowndes County Prison, as we termed our school, with no other treats 'cept graham crackers 'n honey. Now I'm not saying there was anything particularly wrong with school but for a country boy wanting to be outside and doing, any impediment to that desire was an odious and painful torture. It didn't matter that school was over at 2:30 so's to accommodate the farmers who wanted their kids home and helping. For me it represented countless hours wasted in not doing all the necessary things a 6 year-old was obligated to do. I disrecollect just what those obligations were but as memory serves, they were important.

We'd just barely moved to the farm out north of Cat Creek when I started school and I was still smarting from being told that I could not stay at the home we had down near Savannah. All my lifelong friends had been left behind when we traveled those thousands of miles to Cat Creek. Okay, I know it weren't but 150 miles or so but it may as well have been thousands. Automobiles didn't exist at the time, leastways not so anybody would have seen one down in remote-city Georgia. We actually did see one a few years later but that's another story altogether.

Only thing was that move wasn't so bad as I'd expected 'cause there were a couple of boys my age. One feller we called Stinky Shorts became a good friend. He wasn't stinky and I reckon his shorts weren't stinky either but I figure I wouldn't want to investigate that part too closely—then or now. We called him Stinky cause he'd had a losing battle with a skunk a month or so earlier and it took the best part of a couple of weeks before that odor finally abated enough so a body could get near him—if one wanted to. Shorts was his last name and boys being what they are, the nickname stuck. Add to that, he wasn't overly tall for his age so that was a bonus reason for his nickname. About 10 years later that changed in a significant way 'cause he spurted up to 6-foot 4-inches by the time he was a senior in high school. At that size, "Stinky" wasn't a particularly healthy nickname to bandy about.

As I recall he went on to play pro ball for some team up north. Like me, and a great many others like us, he was drafted to go fight the Kaiser over in France. Unlike me, he got through it without even catching a cold. I caught a cold, a couple of bullets, and a whiff or two of that mustard gas. It seems I was destined to be a favorite for catching things most folks would just as soon leave alone. But I could have done without the bullets and mustard gas. Come to think on it, I never have been too thrilled about colds either, given my druthers.

Now Myma was supposed to be coming to us from over in Ray City. Ray City was a pretty ambitious name for a little spot in the road, but even folks in Valdosta knew were it was. Myma had a big old farmhouse up on the west side of Cat Creek. We didn't have a special hold on where the creek went and it did wander on down past us before eventually dumping into the Withlacoochee River near to a mile west of our church. Myma always said she wanted to someday join Albert, her husband, at the church. As a 6 year-old I couldn't understand that 'cause I knew he was in the cemetery right next to the church. When I realized what she was sayin' I said I weren't in no hurry to join anyone in that place, standing or laying down!

Halloween came and went and wasn't anything special for us in those days. We mostly just had some neighbors over and bobbed for apples and played some games. Mama had told us about All Hallow's Eve and had allowed stories about ghosts and han'ts as long as we said right up front they were make believe. But trick-or-treating was something unknown to

19

us. Mama didn't hold to dressin' up and threatening mayhem; said it was against the Bible. Said she'd as soon go to town in Papa's trousers as to follow such nonsense. That's saying something because in my whole life I never ever saw her wear trousers of any kind. She was what a lot of folks would call a proper southern lady and ladies just didn't wear trousers less'n they were proper riding habits—whatever those were.

I do remember one Halloween somebody brought their Ouija board and I'm here to tell you, she threw a fit of an epic magnitude and it took Papa a bit to stop her from tossing that board right into the fire. She made 'em put that thing back in their wagon and promise to never bring it anywhere near our house again. Said it was a tool of Satan just made to look like a fun game. Probably was a good thing they didn't publish horoscopes in the newspapers in those days. I'm sure Mama would have never let a newspaper in the house. She took her Christian duties serious and didn't hold to nothing that even had a hint of heathen thinking.

I kind of wandered off the story a bit but I have to write things down as they come to mind.

Myma was as good as her word. A couple days before Thanksgiving she showed up in her wagon, filled to the top with pots and pans, her flour, seasonings of all sorts and, of course, her cooking tools. Mama didn't say nothing but I saw a bit of frown flit across her face. I suspect she was kind of put out, maybe thinking Myma thought her kitchen tools weren't good enough for Myma to use. In defense of Myma I could kind of understand her wanting to use her own things. She knew them, had her favorites. I know she wasn't bent on being spiteful or anything of that nature. If you do anything like cooking or working in your shop building something or even working on a piece of equipment, you want your own tools to work with no matter if the other feller's are some top of the line brand. You just like what you like and are comfortable with.

I know Myma didn't hold nothing against Mama 'cause she treated Mama like she was her daughter not her daughter-in-law. I overheard her saying that she was sorry Mama'd got stuck with such a no account husband, meaning Papa of course. I was right riled at that but as soon as she'd said it, they both started laughing and Mama said she was working on getting him to be of some account. Only thing was Mama and Papa were both the most upright, honest people I was ever to know and that included Myma. They'd have made a straight back kitchen chair look crooked. I can't remember ever seeing either of them lean back into a chair. As far as Papa went, he was the hardest-working man I ever knew. He'd be out of the house 'fore the sun decided to sneak up out of the Atlantic Ocean and I well remember many times that same sun had gone on to California before he ever came in from the fields. Many a summer day he was still working by moonlight.

The morning after she arrived I asked Myma if she was going to be making The Moon cake. She said she was planning on it as it was the onliest reason she'd come down. She had ordered special new pans from Sears and Roebucks to make one big enough to last all week if we were able to suffer eating on it that long. That was like asking an alligator how many possums it wanted.

Thanksgiving that year was on the 28th of November. I reckon I remember that cause Mama said something about it falling less than a month before Christmas. That sure made this little boy happy. I guess saying most anything about Christmas made this little boy happy. The Tuesday morning before the big day Myma said I had best get on to school and not be getting lost getting home after school if I knew what was good for me. I knew for certain that meant she planned to make the cake that morning. I had my breakfast and rushed off to school with my mouth a watering just thinking about The Moon cake and I reckon the only thing I learned that day was that hours are weeks when your mind is on something that has nothing to do with what you were supposed to be studying on at that moment. I disremember my teacher's name but I do recall she was rather put out at my not paying attention and more'n once she'd called my name four or five times afore she got hold of my wandering mind. That meant I had to stay after school to clean the room and erasers. That was torture 'cause I knew that cake would be gone long before ever I made it home. I reckon that was the day I started calling school the Lowndes County Prison.

As it was I did manage to get it done in what may have been considered record time. Most likely I probably made it home in record time as well. I got near the house and could smell that cake. I knew I'd made it in time. Only thing was, Myma said it first had to cool in the windowsill to let the frosting set for a bit. Then it had to go into the icebox 'cause the weather was still too hot to leave it sittin' out. She may as well of said she could slow time down to make a minute last an hour. I knew that cake'd never cool 'fore Thanksgiving, two days hence! Then I got to smelling something else. Mama had managed to get some time to get into the kitchen and had started working on supper, which was chicken, fried in lard and double dipped in flour to make you slap an angry bull for the last piece. Now I ain't ever slapped a bull, angry or otherwise but considering how good my Mama's chicken was, I figure I could as well have been talked into given it a try…at least once.

Myma had covered the Moon Cake with a piece of linen cloth to keep the tiny flying critters off it as well as the feathered ones. She told us about a blue jay that had flown in one time and landed right in the middle of one of her peach pies and got stuck, ruining the whole pie and not doing the bird no favors either. Said she had to spend half an hour getting all that sticky peach filling off that bird and that as mad as she was about it ruining the pie, she reckoned that bird was just doing what come natural and she didn't have no one to really blame but herself. Said that was when she figured on the linen to reduce the temptation and keep the critters a bit safer. And that worked all right enough 'ceptin for the one time a mama 'coon and six of her little ones smelled peach pie and they all got covered in all that filling 'cause they'd pulled on that linen cloth til they dumped the whole thing on to the ground outside her kitchen window and it landed on top of them babies. She said she was madder'n a wet hen at first and had gone out with a broom to whack them but when she saw all them babies a licken' each other as it they were peach candy, she got to laughing so hard she just couldn't do anything but sit down and watch em. I could understand that cause I've an occasion or two when I was hunting watching how 'coons just seemed to be some of natures clowns as they could sure make you laugh with what they got up to at times. 'Bout the only other critter that seemed to find any and everything amusing were river otters and while there weren't a whole lot in our neck of the woods, we did have a few and I'm saving that story for another time.

I could've sat there just smelling all those kitchen smells and listening to all those kitchen tales but I got shoved out to collect any late eggs I could find. Chickens may not be naturals like 'coons but they could be just as funny. They'd lay their eggs just about any time and I recollect I mentioned it before but them danged birds could find the craziest places to sit down and make their deposit. I'd find eggs in the hog pen, underneath a water trough and I even found 'em up under the front porch. That was kind of a surprise 'cause we had dogs that were pretty good about chasing chickens away from the house.

Long around five o'clock Mama sent my sister Idel to fetch us all in for supper and I wasn't the only one eager to get washed up. We didn't have fried chicken as often as most folks seem to think southern families did. It was a special treat served maybe once a month. First off, you had to have a fair amount of chickens on hand to feed our family at one sitting. With all my siblings and our parents, it was at least a two-chicken meal. Add to that, having enough lard on hand for frying was a bit of a challenge until we raised some hogs a few years later. That was an education for all of us but that's another story. After our experience with hogs, I reckon I understand Jesus sending them demons into that pack of hogs. I suspect he didn't like 'em all that much either!

We all sat down to supper and ate ourselves full of chicken, Mama's amazing biscuits, and some of the green beans my sisters had picked and canned a couple months earlier. Pole beans were just about my favorite green food 'cept maybe white-acre peas but those had to be cooked fresh. For some reason we had rice with the chicken gravy. Rice, too, was a pretty rare dish for us 'cause it had to be store bought and Mama wasn't too crazy on spending money for store bought food. She was of a mind we should eat what we grew. That meant anything that could be canned in the fall would be what we'd be getting until spring 'cept what may still be available such as potatoes or squash. I recollect some of the conversation that evening touched on how uncommon late it was for the spuds and squashes to be growing still.

We'd all pretty much hurried through supper as we were anticipating The Moon cake for dessert. I'd done some serious damage to a meal made up of my favorites but I'll admit to holding a little bit of room for that cake.

Myma went into the kitchen to fetch the cake and we could hear her fussing around and mutterin'. We thought she was trying to get our taste buds primed and were laughing about that when she came out with a confused look on her face and said, "It's done gone!"

You could have told me Abe Lincoln was standing at the door and I wouldn't have been more surprised or shocked. We all ran into the kitchen, 'cept Papa of course as I reckon it just didn't seem proper for him to be showing too much surprise at anything that happened on the farm. We all looked. High, low, and places Myma might have missed but The Moon cake, along with the cake dish it had occupied was indeed done gone.

The last I'd seen it was when it sat cooling on the windowsill over the kitchen sink. With the wisdom of a 6-year old, I speculated some critter had grabbed it away. Alas, the screen on the window was still closed and latched.

After all that searching and worrying, we trudged back to the dining table to try to figure out the mystery while we had a make-believe dessert of cookies and ice cold milk—good, but not what we were hoping for. Everyone voiced a theory but Papa would only agree that it was indeed a mystery. He had, he said, been suspicious since Halloween. Myma gave him a funny look like she wasn't sure what he was thinking but she snapped her mouth shut and wouldn't guess any more.

Papa was sure, he said, something had been sneaking around the farm. He'd noticed things go missing but find them later someplace where they shouldn't have been. Said he thought there might be ha'nts cause of all we'd been doing at Halloween. Mama shushed him on that and said there wasn't such things as ha'nts and even if there were, why'd they steal something like The Moon cake. She'd never heard of ghosts having a sweet tooth then she surprised us all by agreeing with my guess that it was probably a 'coon or 'possum that took the cake. Only thing was, a 'coon or 'possum would have made an awful mess. But a bear could have shoved the whole cake in his mouth at once and not leave a crumb for us to find. It had to be a bear. But would a bear eat the plate and latch the window screen and leave no tracks?

Mama gave Mel and me several pretty suspicious looks but we'd been inside most of the time so she must have figger'd we hadn't had an opportunity to sneak off with a cake.

Late that night Mel started jerking on my arm to wake me up. I reckon I'd gone off to sleep pretty hard and fast 'cause of not having any extra sugar from the cake,.

"Listen" he whispered hoarsely. "Do you hear something out by the chicken pen?" I listened for a minute or so and sure'nuff, I heard a kind of screeching sound like something was being dragged across a piece of steel or a roofing panel. I remember the hairs on my neck must have heard it too 'cause they were standing up and listening pretty danged hard.

"You go see what it is Mel and I'll keep a lookout from the window."

"You're crazy Herman if you think I'm going out there by myself. If something getting chickens is making that kind of noise, it's welcome to 'em."

"Mel, I can see them chickens ain't the only thing with feathers around here. Come on, let me get my boots on and we'll both go see what the heck's going on."

With that, we managed to slide out the window quiet like so's to not wake anyone else in the house. When you think about it that was about the dumbest thing a body could do when he's a hunting ha'nts. Later, not much later but too much later, I figured what we shouldda done was raise a ruckus and get as many folks involved as was available so the ha'nts couldn't get us without a struggle but I wasn't thinking clear at the time.

Mel had been so excited he'd forgot to put his britches on and the only thing he was wearing beside his shirt and boots was his underpants which sure should have scared any ghost if there was one. I took one look at him and got to chuckling so hard I reckon I'd have survived meeting up with just about anything 'cept maybe Papa.

We rounded the corner of the pen when we saw the dark shadow of a man and knew it was a chicken thief. Without thinking on it both Mel and I rushed up and jumped on him to keep him from stealing any more chickens. He hollered and started swinging not sure what was happening. It didn't take long to knock two little boys off his back and Papa just sat down right there and asked us what in the world we thought we were doing. I told him we thought he was the one who had stolen The Moon cake and had come back for chickens.

He was laughing pretty good at that and said he'd better learn to not go out to cover up the chicken pen at night 'cause of a storm coming. And, maybe he'd better put a lock on our window to prevent us from escaping as well. He wasn't mad at us but he sure was surprised that we'd been willing to tackle anything in the dark. Said it was brave of us to do that but we shouldn't ever do it again cause it might for sure be somebody trying to steal chickens and if a person was desperate enough to do that, they wouldn't think too much on hurting a couple of little boys. Said if we heard something again to come wake him up and he'd do the "investigating".

But that still didn't solve the mystery of The Moon cake and it remained a mystery for a long time. Myma wasn't about to admit defeat and she was in the kitchen right after breakfast the next morning and made two cakes that looked like The Moon. Said she wasn't taking chances on something, ha'nt or otherwise getting away with another one. She also made some divinity fudge which I learned later took a whole lot of effort and a heap of talent to do. We had ham that night and everyone got all The Moon cake we could eat. Not all we wanted, just what we could eat. That cake was so rich it'd make a hobo a millionaire were he to have half a slice. We couldn't even think about the divinity until the next day.

I reckon it must have been just before Papa left us to have a conversation with St Peter that I finally learned the truth about the haunts stealing The Moon cake. Papa had slowed down a great deal by then and we were all sitting around visiting one evening when Papa said he reckoned the time'd come to tell us something important. Oh, not how he wanted to be buried or who was to get his favorite shotgun. He wanted to tell us about the night the ha'nts stole The Moon cake.

"You boys darned near ruined the whole secret when you jumped me that night. I'd met a feller down the road who was running on pretty hard times. He'd had a pretty decent little farm down across state line and if you remember, that was the year we had that heavy rain come through in August. What we got out of that storm wasn't nothing to what that fella got and it wiped out his whole crop of tobacco. It was the second year of crop failure for him so he'd lost his farm to the bank and to taxes. It just 'bout killed him to go on the road trying to salvage his life and dignity. He'd sent his wife and a their two boys back to her folks for the time being and he'd gone out looking for work. I wasn't in any position to hire on anyone at the moment but I wasn't going to let a man go hungry. I promised to keep his secret and told him to stay down in the hay-loft that night and I'd figure something out. Well, Myma had just made that cake and as I was walking back in, without even thinking about it, I grabbed it and took it down to him. Told him to sit tight, I'd get him some other eating's later on. I never did figure out why I took that cake. I know eating too much of it makes a body sick. Well, he did eat a fair chunk of it and said he'd appreciated it but that whole cake was more'n he could handle. I'd just taken him a sack of your mothers cornbread and a couple pieces of chicken you mongrels hadn't eaten and given him the name of a feller I knew over in Hahira who was looking for some help.

"Turns out, he not only got on with my friend but he ended up owning the whole deal several years later when my friend died. He brought his wife and family back and if you will remember, we used to get a big ham every year from the hardware store. He said I saved his life that night but I kept trying to tell him, he saved himself. Hard work and moral living is what saved his life. I just happened to be there for an evening.

"So, now you know. Your mother never knew. This is all news to her as well. Ain't but this one thing I ever kept from her, or any of you for that matter. You boys landing on me that night scared a couple years off me and that feller too but I'm still proud of what you thought you were doing.

"You just remember, our obligation to the Lord is not a once-a-week event. Remember there are always folks worse off than you are and they might only need a piece of cake or a glass of water.

And I'm grateful that the Lord saw fit to use me for something besides hollering at you kids and cussin' at a broken plow.

"Come to think of it, there was one person I did tell. All my life Myma knew when I'd been up to something. I never could keep a secret from her."

With that, we all got up and headed to the dining table. See, Mama had made a dessert no one turns down—The Moon cake.

MISTER LONGFORTH

One year we had an old fella come riding up in an old wagon that looked like it had come clear from California and turns out it shore had. The back and the sides were held in place with leather straps and even some bailing wire in a couple of places. He was using an old iron cot as a seat on that thing. We saw him coming up the road from a long way off and I think it was half an hour before he finally pulled up at our place. "Howdy" he said. "You folks mind if I fill up my jugs and give my mules a rest for a bit?"

Well them mules already looked about as rested as a dog on the porch but Papa said come on ahead and he'd help fill his jugs. The feller said his name was Samuel Longforth and that he was heading home to Valdosta to die. This took us all off guard as you can imagine. Papa asked him what he meant by "heading home to die".

"Well, young'n (we snickered at that as he was talking to Papa), I been gone for nigh on 65 years. Spent most of my life in a place called Oregon out east of Portland a couple hundred miles or so and I saw more gold there than any of them fellers in Californee ever did and I'm here to swear to that. Oh, I spent time in Californee but wild folks seemed to foller the gold and it got so crowded I worked my way up to the Oregon country. I got my share of what I need and then just started heading east in this old wagon and I ain't really stopped yet. I knew one day, like all of us, I'd be standing at the Pearly Gates and sure hopin' I'd be going in. I'd read somewhere about them African elephants knowing when they was going to die and they had a special place for it and when their time was near, they'd just start heading that way. I figured I was getting close to going myself and my special place is where I was born and that's why it's taken me all this time to get back. See, I warn't in no hurry."

He stayed with us for about a week and even showed us some gold nuggets in a little pouch with fine grains of sand. Only it wasn't sand but gold dust. He'd lived off his findings his whole adult life and said he had no regrets and no apologies to make 'ceptin to the Lord for taking so long. Said he was saving the rest for a fine casket and a funeral. He was the genuine article and he showed us kids how to cook over a fire out by his wagon and how to start fires if you didn't have a match and a lot of other things but, I'm sad to say, I've forgotten most of it.

Mister Longforth must have taken what I called the scenery route to Valdosta from our place. It was another nine months 'fore we heard he had passed on. The newspaper said he was 89 and that he'd outlived 4 wives and half a dozen children. It said he had 18 children in all from them wives but ain't none of them lived in Georgia so he'd had no one to speak for him when he died. He'd left instruction with an undertaker down there on his wants and he seemed to have gotten what he wanted. He had a fine big headstone and it had the day he was born, his name and a note at the bottom that read "Home At Last". We paid a visit and put some flowers on his grave when we were down there a couple months later. Always wondered what things he saw all those years and in all those places. I ain't so sure but if he'd kept on going, he'd still be here today and that was 60 some odd years ago!

One thing I always wondered about him was that he was the only Longforth I ever heard of in Valdosta and I did a bit of looking. I'm sure he was right and considering how long he'd been gone, whatever folks he'd had there must have moved on before they started keeping any kind of serious records of who's who.

For some reason I got to thinking about him one day a few years later as I was sitting in a trench over in France and I added up or rather subtracted some things and it was then I realized he'd have been born when some of those Founding Fathers were still around and that's some kind of history when you think about it. Just made a body realize this country hadn't really been around all that long after all and I reckon my thinking on him was realizing how long France, England and all them European countries had been around.

It made me proud to think about that sad looking Old Glory we had strung up in camp and the things us "young'ns" had managed to do. Not to say some things were not without a bit of ugliness. I don't reckon any country, young or old ain't got something in it's background that folks would kind of like to forget and ain't proud of. Still, I figure ain't been but one perfect man on this old ball and He got killed for His troubles. But He showed He was a tellin' the truth when He didn't stay in that tomb for long. I'm sad to say there ain't been nothing but arguing over that fact since then…some for good and some for not so noble reasons. Even so, I am pleased and proud to be called "American".

THELMA AND THE WORMS

Thelma, my youngest sister by some years, was born during a thunderstorm. If you ask folks about babies born at that time, you'll hear all kinds of tales of it being good, bad, or something else. For us, it just was. Thunderstorms in Georgia ain't nothing special, particularly during the summer and most of us got so we almost prayed for one around 4 or so in the afternoon to cool the day a bit and to provide a little cooler sleeping weather. For most of my life, air conditioning was something unheard of. For a farmer at the end of the nineteenth century, it just didn't exist. Didn't exist anywhere else at that time either I reckon. Regardless, Thelma was born and we all just took it as a matter of course that in a few years we'd have another hand to help around the house. But we knew that, in the meantime, we were gonna have a lot of noisy nights and unpleasant smells. That had nothing to do with Thelma specifically, it just kind of went along with her being a newborn.

Life went along pretty normal for the next couple of years and it was when Thelma turned three or maybe four, that we got a taste of just how different from the rest of us she was. That's nothing either, as we were all pretty different from one another but Thelma had a determined streak none of us could match and if she made up her mind about it, there wasn't anything anybody could do to change that mind; including getting swatted with a hickory switch. She wouldn't cry though and I think that frustrated Mama to no end. She'd swat her three or four times and Thelma would just stand there and her lips would turn purple with the pain. When it was over she'd just walk away and not say nothing to nobody for the rest of the day.

I reckon I need to clarify a bit about how Mama and Papa handed out discipline. All of us boys got the end of a piece of leather and I don't mean the good end either but it was a rare occurrence and probably well deserved. But Papa never laid a hand on my sisters. He left that to Mama to deal with and she was less shy about "educating" the girls than Papa was about reshaping our attitudes. I think that's cause Mama was but a slip of a woman and she must have felt she had more need to motivate the girls than Papa did us boys. Anyway, with either of them, physical discipline was rare, swift, and done with in short order. Nothing was said afterwards and we got on with life. I can only recollect 4 times that Papa felt the need to "reeducate" me. At the time, I probably thought once was more than enough.

Thelma must have been four, because her vocabulary was fairly good at that time and she already knew her ABC's and could count as high as you'd care to let her. Anyway, one afternoon in the late spring, Thelma was out by the creek with Mel and you could hear them laughing and splashing around. That creek wasn't much to look at as I've said before but you could find a hole or two enough to drown a feller if you worked at it. And if you were careful you could pull some decent pan fish out of those holes too, and nothing worked better for bait than a juicy fat worm squirming on a hook.

It was getting on late in the day and you could see thunderheads building up in the west and starting to head our way, so Mama hollered for me to go get Mel and Thelma and bring them home. I'd been working on a new axe handle for Papa. Truth be told, I'd likely be the one on the working end of it. I'd found a good chunk of pecan wood and it worked most as well as hickory and besides, pecan was much more common.

I put the soon-to-be-handle up and headed on over to get 'em and grouse at 'em for making me stop what I was doing to go round 'em up.

I reached the creek about 20 minutes before that storm hit and found Thelma was on the other side. She was down on her knees in the mud and I hollered for her to grab her stuff and get home. She hollered back she was still grabbing up worms and that it must be because of the storm as they were everywhere. Well that didn't set well with me and I didn't waste no time in making it clear she was to grab her can of worms and get home. She just yelled and said I was mean and didn't want her to have no fun but she did get her can and cane pole then joined Mel and me to run back to the house. It wasn't a minute after we got inside when those clouds burst and it came pouring down rain. Thelma ran out the back door and put her can of worms underneath the steps back of the house to keep 'em from drowning and to keep the chickens from having a feast at her expense. As we were dragging Thelma back inside I heard Papa holler from the barn that he'd just stay there 'til the rain had let up a bit.

That may sound like Papa didn't want to get wet but those thunder showers in the south could drown a whale in about 2 minutes. And that doesn't include all the wind, the lightening and thunder that goes along with it. I've been in rain in a lot of places, including England and France and places here in this country as well and nothing beats a summer thunderstorm in the south. So you can forgive Papa for not wanting to rush to the house.

Papa had seen a barn get hit by lightening one time and said that barn just exploded. Said anything that powerful deserved respect and he'd made sure the house, barn, and all the various outbuildings had lightening rods on them. Besides that, Papa was not one to be seen running for or from anything. He and I had a memory a few years later but that's for another time.

Well, that storm turned into one of those all night affairs for the most part. It let up enough around 6 for Papa to get back to the house with my brothers Fred and Alton. Said a little water never hurt nothing but I suspect he didn't want to cross the yard until the lightening had died down a bit. He wouldn't admit to being afraid of if but I can tell you he never gave it a chance to get the better of him. I reckon anybody ain't a little afraid of lightening is someone you might want to keep your eyes on, cause that ain't normal.

We all stayed up pretty late that night and I saw Thelma sneak out the back door a couple of times. She said she was just checking to make sure her worms were alright. I thought that was kind of weird but at four she'd just started learning about fishing and was afraid her newfound bait would be gone before morning.

That storm must have had a whole bunch of kin folks with it as it kept a rumbling pretty much all night and when we did get to bed, it had not only cooled off but had almost gotten cold. Folks tend to forget that those rain storms start from way up high and it's pretty darned cold in them clouds and those rain drops don't get a lot of chance to warm up before they hit the ground. Last thing I remember that night is how comfortable it was as far as sleeping weather goes and I nodded off almost as soon as I crawled into bed.

Along about 6 the next morning, I woke up to the sounds of Papa holleingr and swearing, which for him was danged rare. Papa didn't use bad language much and Mama never. Papa had slipped out the back door to use the facilities and had accidentally kicked that can of worms. Well, those worms turned out to be a whole bunch of baby water moccasins and when he hit that can, they scattered underneath him.

Weren't none of them bigger than 4 or 5 inches long but Papa knew what they were and when I got to the door, he was dancing around and slapping the ground with the shovel he'd managed to grab. There must have been 20 or so and between him dancing around, slapping them with the shovel and Thelma hollering to not kill her worms, Mama almost fainted. She was relieved none of them had bit Thelma but angry that she'd brought home what Papa later described as a can of Death. I do remember Thelma actually bawled for over an hour about losing her bait and her fear at hearing Papa swearing.

Mama didn't switch her for that but I know Mel got "talked" to about not watching out for Thelma. When Papa had finally calmed down enough to not have a crack in his voice he asked her where she'd been and how she'd come to have a can of snakes. Poor Thelma had no idea they were snakes and only thought them to be big earthworms. She said she thought they looked kind of funny but at four, she'd not realized the difference.

Mama asked him if he wanted a cup of coffee and he just said he didn't reckon he'd need any that morning. I don't know if Mama ever said anything about his cursing. She may have been guilty of muttering a word or two under her breath and knew there were times when nothing else would do. I'm sure the next words out of her mouth were prayers of gratitude that one of those little snakes didn't grab on to the end of one of Thelma's fingers. She knew a little snake is often more deadly than a big one.

Papa grabbed a shovel and a can of kerosene then Mel showed him where they'd been digging. I thought back to what I'd been reading in school about Russia's "scorched earth" philosophy in her fight agin' that Napoleon feller. Well, Papa pretty much did the same thing to those moccasins.

He burned the fishing hole and everything around it, plus an old dead oak tree and two live pine trees to boot. Just ruined that fishing hole for sure and for good. I found out later my Papa could deal with a mean mule or bad bull but he detested snakes...moccasins in particular.

Like I said early on, Thelma had kind of a stubborn streak about her but she wasn't born in the shallow end of the gene pool either. Once she learned something, she never forgot it. She got over the killing of all her "worms" and as she aged she got to be darned good at finding real worms. She never again picked up one off the ground though. Said worms had to be found underground. Afore long she could out dig and out fish most any-body.

I guess I take after Papa...I couldn't abide snakes as a young'un...still can't. But I remember talking to Thelma years later about those "worms" and she just shook her head and said it didn't matter, worms or snakes were all the same to a fish. And she never did seem to be afraid of snakes even after that incident. In fact, I can't think of much that really bothered Thelma. Maybe being born during a thunderstorm, sorta tempered what shoulda been natural-born fears.

Even as a young'un she was not afraid to speak her mind. That exasperated Mama on more than a few occasions and I remember one time seeing Papa walk away with a kind of a wry smile on his face after hearing Thelma express some pretty strong views on boys. She wasn't but 11 or 12 at the time. She had a crush on a boy but he wasn't having a thing to do with her…any girls for that matter. Couple of years later he changed his mind but it was too late as far as Thelma was concerned. They never did have a meeting of the minds.

CHRISTMAS IN 1905

When I turned 10 in October all the world had been abuzz about the Wright Brothers and their flying machine for a couple of years already. We had a cousin living up in the North Carolina who had actually seen the machine and she'd come down to visit over the past summer. She hadn't actually seen it fly but we were pretty excited to know someone who had seen any part of that famous event. She told us about watching them haul the machine back over the river and load it up to get it back home. I was amazed.

Of course by 1905 the Sears and Roebuck Christmas catalog had new flying-machine toys—guaranteed to fly—that you could put together yourself. We were all desperate to get one for Christmas. Hints were the best you could offer when you wanted something. A sure way to not get what you wanted was to actually ask for it. Mama was pretty strict when it came to Christmas gifts. She took the view it wasn't very Christian to just right out say what you wanted. 'sides missing the whole point of the day...it was for the giving of gifts not for "shopping" for toys. So we had to resort to subtle hints. Understand, "subtle" and "10-year-old-boy" are exclusive concepts. I was about as subtle as the bull our neighbor had looking at our cows but at least I didn't beller about it as he did.

Thanksgiving had come and gone and we were all looking forward to Christmas as was usually the case. We weren't what folks'd call prosperous farmers but we weren't starving either. Papa worked the farm pretty hard and we were comfortable enough but there wasn't a whole lot extra and that's pretty much the way it was with most folks we knew. You simply lived task to task and day to day. There wasn't ever any thought about building up a nest egg or something as ridiculous as retirement. All of the kids I knew helped their folks on their farms same as we did. I guess all that working and making do is what made a lot of city folks think we were poor.

Only thing was, we didn't know we were supposed to be poor. But it didn't matter 'cause we had food, a comfortable house, and decent clothes to wear. The weather was pretty mild in the region so we didn't wear our shoes much during the summers though you'd not be thought too smart if you took off without them come winter. As a result, we usually only had a pair of new shoes show up every other year or so and they all went to the older kids. That meant some of us didn't ever get the new ones at all but the worn ones handed down from somebody else. If they were too badly worn Papa would take 'em over to a cobbler in Hahira to get 'em "reshod". That meant they got new soles and maybe new laces and a bit of buffing up.

Papa would use something until there was nothing possible to salvage from it. He wasn't what you'd call cheap but I once heard a feller tell him he may not be a Scotsman but he was sure leaning over that border pretty hard. It was years later when I understood that was a reference to how frugal the Scots are reputed to be. I was sitting in a trench over in France and when I learned that bit of lore. I started chuckling and then I laughed so hard the sergeant thought I was having a fit and was fixing to slug me to bring me to my senses. I told him I was fine, just finally "got" an old joke from 10 years before.

So back to Christmas in 1905. Mama had been warning us to not expect too much for presents that year as the tobacco crop had not brought near as much as Papa had hoped and like as not he'd have to sell a couple of cows to keep things going. That kind o' scared us as we had only 10 of 'em and of course we'd named every one. That meant they weren't just farm animals but pets as far as we were concerned. Papa didn't say anything about it but he did seem kind of surprised when we confronted him. My sister Idel was a year older than I was and, right up front she said he'd better not sell Loraine as she was her favorite and Loraine would never understand being taken away from her family. I said a cow didn't think about family that way and a cow'd be fine as long as she got her food and a place to bed down no matter where she was. I thought Idel was going to hit me when Mel, my younger brother spoke up, worried they'd sell Bob and I just shook my head. We don't know why he picked that name but wouldn't budge on it even though we kept telling him Bob was a boy's name and not a name for a cow. He said it didn't matter. He'd named her Bob 'cause every time he went out to roust them into the pasture that cow would bob her head up and down.

I'd named one cow Methane 'cause that's what she gave us all the time. Papa heard what I'd named her and he chuckled a good bit but said I couldn't call her that around Mama. She'd have busted my britches if she'd heard it. He suggested if I shortened it to Messy I'd be okay. I don't remember the other cow's names but I reckon it don't matter much. When you had Methane, Loraine, and Bob, the other names didn't matter too much I suppose.

One thing I do remember about Methane was her straying into Mama's garden. Mama was hollering at her and pushing her from behind when Methane lived up to her name and Mama got a strong smell that results from moving a northbound cow further north—from the south end. She wrinkled up her nose, whacked poor Methane in the rump with the backside of a garden rake and shouted 'bout no self-respecting cow's got any business behaving that way. We wanted to laugh but quickly recognized laughter as an unsafe reaction on our part, so we just grabbed Methane and led her out to the pasture as quick as we could.

Christmas was moving closer and closer and since there wasn't a whole lot that escaped a body on a farm, I knew Mama hadn't ordered anything from the Sears and Roebuck's Christmas catalog. I was sorely frustrated at that. I wanted one of those Wright flyers so bad it was all I could do to keep from coming out and asking for it.

I had gone to the barn a few days before to try to build one from memory and from a picture I'd seen in a magazine months before. I can't say I was making any progress. Those Yankee boys may have had one up on a dumb farm boy from Georgia but I wasn't discouraged, just frustrated. I figured I just hadn't got something quite right yet. I saw Papa watching me from the farm wagon on his way down to get some firewood he'd stacked up down in the woods. I asked him why we didn't bring all that wood up and stack it by the house so he told me a story about a woodpile fire next to some folks' house down in Hahira. Until he could get a proper shed built out by the barn, the bulk of the wood would stay down by the creek. I know he'd seen what I was doing but he didn't say anything. That was one of those subtle hints I was mentioning earlier. Well, he kept on going to gather the wood and I'd swear I saw kind of a grin on him. Maybe that was just wishful thinking.

Like it always does, Christmas morning arrived on time and we kids were up before the chickens had gone to bed the night before. We all sneaked down the hall snickering and whispering about how to get Mama and Papa up. One thing was an absolute in our house--no one was allowed into the parlor before the folks were up. No excuse was accepted and while we were all sorely tempted to peek we'd learned long ago when Papa, or Mama, said no excuses, it meant no excuses would be accepted. Their bedroom door was closed and we could see there was a piece of paper on the door. Turned out it was a sign. Written in scraggly handwriting was a message: BEARS HYBERNATING, DISTURBING THEM WILL BE HAZARDOUS TO YOUR HEALTH.

We all started snickering at that and I reckon snickering children ain't exactly quiet. About a minute later, the door burst open and Papa came storming out growling and grabbing at whoever was too close. That happened to be Mel. Poor Mel went to hollering and screaming and Mama came out pretty quick and told Papa to not be eating no children til he'd had his coffee first. Mel stopped screaming at that and started giggling so hard and squirming so bad that Papa had to let him go afore he dropped him. Said he didn't like chewing on little kids anyway. Said the bones got stuck in his teeth.

With that, we pushed and pulled them into the parlor, fussing 'cause they were so slow. Mel kept begging Papa to growl again but I reckon that was a short-lived bit of melodrama for him 'cause he just wouldn't do it. Papa had a hidden sense of silliness that was never obvious. If you weren't watching close when it popped out you'd miss it all together. Then you'd have to wait and hope to see the next one that went sneaking by. We got them into the parlor at last to see what Santa had left us. I had been telling Mel I strongly suspected I'd be getting that aeroplane and I looked all over for a present with my name on it. I knew it had to be there even if my hints hadn't been as obvious as they might have been. But it wasn't. I found presents from Mama and Papa and from all my siblings--socks and such. There were a couple of presents from Santa that were in a Sears and Roebuck box but all those packages were the wrong size so I didn't even open them.

Frustrated at being denied, I was sitting there watching the others and my dismay must have been obvious 'cause Papa asked me what the matter was. I couldn't tell him, could I. So I just shrugged and said I reckon Santa hadn't got my letter after all. Papa grinned and said I should learn to be more patient and to remember some of Santa's gifts might not fit under the tree. Some might be behind it or even in some other place. With that, I ran back over to look behind the tree but Papa stopped me. Said if I was going to look there, I should first open the presents I'd ignored. Again I shrugged and said okay. I could endure the process of opening the gifts I knew would be boring when it meant I'd be opening my aeroplane next. I picked up one of the gifts I'd ignored and realized it was pretty heavy for a model aeroplane.

I was stunned to find a full case of 12-gauge shotgun shells. The next one was a new gun cleaning kit. I almost knocked down the tree running around it. Against the wall leaned a present shaped just like a broom all wrapped up. I didn't have to guess. I knew what it was and boy was I right. It was a single-shot 12-gauge shotgun, polished to a shine and clean as a whistle, but not from the Sears and Roebuck's Christmas catalog. I asked Papa about that.

"Son, I had a conversation with Santa and asked him to send down a box of shells. Told him we'd provide the rest."

He never did tell where he'd got the gun but I didn't care 'cause Santa came through in a way I'd never have thought he could. It was a total surprise and that made Mama sigh. I reckon Santa knows what you truly want rather than what you thought you wanted. I'd never dreamed of being lucky enough to get a shotgun anytime soon.

As a surprise to Mel I bought him the model aeroplane the following Christmas. It was a new model, improved on what the Misters Wright had first flown. He spent the better part of a month out in the barn putting it together. He flew it twice and it flew well enough. But Ralph, our Rhode Island Red rooster didn't seem to be amused by the competition. When Mel made the mistake of landing it too close to the hen house Ralph customized it. It no longer resembled an aircraft. The bird put an end to the Misters Williams' adventures into aeronautics.

About 15 years later I was sitting in a trench over in France watching those flyboys going over. I realized I'd completely forgotten my desire for a little model aeroplane. But I put that gun to good use for many years. It became even more special when my dog Stoney came along to help me find quail. That little gun even collected a few deer. I saved the box the first shells came in and gave it to one of my grandsons many years ago. In those days, shells came in small wooden crates and while I've had many cases of shells over the years, that little box was my first one. I used it for storing most about anything for a long time. I still have that shotgun though it's glory days are long past. It hangs above the mantle to remind me sometimes Santa can surprise a body.

STONEY

The day before my 10th birthday Papa was in a pretty foul mood. Seems one of the blades on the plow had snapped off and he'd called the farm store over in Hahira, where he'd bought it, to get another blade. The feller at the store told him he didn't have any in stock, he'd have to order it and that's the second reason for Papa turning foul.

Now, in those days farm stores in small towns couldn't afford to keep a lot of things on the shelf and it wasn't uncommon that things had to be ordered through the mail. The feller told Papa he could have it shipped straight to us but it would take a couple weeks at best. He offered to check around and see if he could find one somewhere. Half an hour later he called back. He'd talked to his brother down in Valdosta who had not just one but two. Papa said to call his brother back and tell him to hold both of them and that he'd drive down to Valdosta and get them both.

Let me explain about driving anywhere in 1905. There were cars of course. I reckon Atlanta probably had dozens but down in our end of the country they were few and far between. So "driving" meant hitching the horses to a wagon and tearing down the road at a breakneck speed of two or maybe even 4 miles per hour...if you had a downhill run. And, while Hahira was 7 miles away, Valdosta was just a mite over 20. That meant a trip to Valdosta was pretty much a two-day event.

By this time it had just slipped past 9 in the morning and Mel and I went out to the barn to help hitch up the wagon. Papa said he'd stay with Orlee and her husband that night and start back in the morning. Orlee was one of my older sisters who'd married a pharmacist fella and they'd moved to Valdosta a couple years before.

Papa was just pulling out when Mama called out to hold him up and she gave him a list of some things he could pick up for the house since he was going to the big city anyway. She'd sneaked a reminder on the list that my birthday was the next day and he should bring me something special.

Shortly after supper the next evening we heard him coming up the road and he seemed to be in a pretty good mood when he pulled in front of the barn. I thought that kind of odd him losing two good days of farm work and all. That meant something with it coming up to winter. I reckon it means something any time, now that I consider it.

Mama had made one of those chocolate cakes with coconut sprinkled all over it. The special treat was we all got to pitch in making peach ice cream. There was no store-bought ice cream in those days so, if you was rich enough and had a source of ice, you had an ice cream maker and you did your own in whatever flavor you wanted. I purely loved peach ice cream and even today, there ain't nothing better than homemade peach ice cream, especially if you have fresh peaches right off the tree.

That time, they were preserved peaches, it being October and peaches had been picked, peeled and put up for several months. I didn't care about that. To me, it was pure heaven. I'd have eaten the whole lot had my siblings dared turn their backs. We were just finishing up and I was looking at all the things I got for my birthday and thinking all was pretty alright with the world as far as I was concerned.

Most of the things were nothing special. Mel gave me a pocketknife he'd found down towards Cat Creek. You could tell it'd been there a while as it had a couple spots of rust on it but Mel had cleaned it up fairly well and it worked just fine as far as I was concerned. Idell and Thelma had made some stocking caps and even two pair of socks for winter-wear. I say winter-wear 'cause that's when we wore shoes. Come summertime we mostly went bare footed.

Papa came in with a couple boxes of things Mama had asked for and told Mel and me to go unhitch the wagon and take care of the horses. He didn't say much else except'n he was hungry and tired and just wanted to go sit down and have a pull on his pipe.

Mel and I took off to the barn to take care of the wagon and horses. We pushed the wagon into the barn and fed the horses, taking care to see that they were rubbed down and settled. We'd started back to the house when I heard something kind of peculiar in the wagon. I figgered it was just one of the half-dozen or so barn cats chasing after a mouse. I hopped up in the wagon to watch it catch the mouse only there wasn't no cat. Instead, the whining, mewing sound was coming from up under the seat.

I reached in under the seat and dragged out a little box. Danged if there wasn't a dog in it…a puppy actually. Well, I grabbed that pup and tore off for the house to tell Papa he had a hitchhiker in the wagon and held him up to show 'im. Papa just smiled and said "Happy Birthday Son. You got yerself a Gorden Setter". I'll tell you, all the gold in Spain couldn't have made me happier.

I'd been asking for a dog to help me with bird hunting. Papa had given me a used single shot 12 gauge the Christmas before and I'd go out as often as I could hunting rabbits and squirrels and wishing I had a dog for hunting quail. We had quail running all over the place but a feller just couldn't sneak up of those little critters no matter how hard he tried. They was the skiddaliest things a body ever come up on. Only turkey seems worse and trying to get close enough to get a shot one of those was nigh impossible.

Now if you're asking what the heck is a 9 year old boy doing with a shotgun, you have to remember times were different back then If you were big enough to not get knocked down by the recoil, you were old enough to hunt and any meat you brought in helped feed the family.

I went to bed that night a hugging and petting on that poor little puppy til he probably figgered I was gonna rub his fur right off and when he started crying about it I put him up under my blanket and he curled right up and went to sleep. That was fine with me until about two o'clock when he stood up and relieved himself right on the bed!

I was as mad as a new hen in the coop and I promise, that's mad. I kept jumping on and off the bed and finally pulled the sheeting off and dumped it all on the floor. I grabbed that pup and stuffed his little nose down in what he'd done. He sure was scared by my tone and just hunkered down and whimpered. Well, I got to feeling pretty poor about that and figured he didn't know any better and started petting him and talking low and soft to him. He just sighed, curled up and went back to sleep. I could tell it was no real matter to him and I curled up on the bedding on the floor as well.

I must have dozed off pretty hard 'cause the next thing I know the sun's up and Mama's calling for us to rise and shine and then she's fussing at me to come get the dog out of the kitchen…fast. I ran in, grabbed him up and lit out for the barn.

I found a piece of rope and tied it around his neck and pretty much dragged him around the farm for about an hour. I'll tell you he sure didn't like that rope and I was kind of at a loss as to what to do when Papa came out of the barn and handed me a strap of leather he'd cut off an old harness. He'd punched holes in it and found an old buckle and sewed it on to the strap. That durn collar was 'bout as big as the dog but Papa said to just put it on him and give him some time and he'd soon grow into it. The pup must have understood 'cause he just sniffed it then seemed to think it was okay. I let him loose in the barn for a bit and he ran around like he was wearing the Crown Jewels. That is if the Crown Jewels was made out of old cowhide that smelled like an old wet mule and was four times to big. He tripped over the extra length half a dozen times and we were laughing fit to bust.

After a few dozen trips around the barn he pulled up short and just froze, looking up at one of the horse stalls. Perched on the top rail was an old cat one of my sisters had named Buttercup. Well I'm here to tell you that was probably the most misnamed cat you ever met. Buttercup had established a reputation around the farm as the meanest, ill-tempered critter a body ever ran across. She had one torn ear and had been born with a tail about half the length of a normal cat. Papa was sure her daddy was an old bobcat 'cause there ain't nothing in the woods meaner than a bobcat.

All I know is she was eyeing my brand new puppy like it was an oversized rat and from what we could tell, she was a gauging how far she'd have to jump to get him. Pup just stood there a looking at her and her a looking right back and that stumpy tail a swishing back and forth…pretty fast at first but then it slowed and finally stopped.

Before any of us could get there, she'd jumped down and landed about six inches in front of that pup. The crazy thing was that the pup never moved. He just stood there frozen, watching Buttercup. Old Buttercup must have been confused 'cause before when she jumped at something it'd take off like the devil hisself was after them and with that cat, that wasn't far from true. Pup though, just stood there while Buttercup hissed and spit. Still no reaction from the pup. Then Buttercup raised up straight and stalked off. Right then I knew that pup's name and I called out "Stonewall come on over here." Cause that's what he'd been, a stone wall. He must have figured that's what he needed… a name, 'cause he just turned and came a bouncing and a tripping over to me as happy as a pup could be.

Stonewall never seemed afraid of anything. I suppose being that close to death that morning, he must have decided there wasn't much else to worry about. As for Buttercup, she was never the same after that, not so much nicer but just a little less mean. Got so folks could ALMOST pet her, still risky, but she'd actually grown worse towards the other pets on the farm. Maybe she was trying to protect her reputation as a Bad Cat.

Stonewall lost his formal name the next spring. Hollering "Stonewall" just seemed too much mouthing so I changed it to Stoney. We were great friends for many years. Stoney took to bird hunting with very little training. He came to pointing and retrieving like he'd been studying for it. He'd run down a rabbit if he got half a chance and he purely loved finding quail. I had other dogs over the years and I loved 'em all, but there was only one Stoney. Sitting here writing about him, I'm kind of getting a little mournful and miss him still. I reckon a boy's first dog is the one he loves most. I know I was blessed to have shared some time on this old rock with him.

That first "accident" in the bed was the last one. I reckon he didn't appreciate being fussed at and there was never a repeat.

Dogs, boys, and guns. Nothing better.

STONEWALL
(WHAT WE LEARNED ABOUT CHICKENS)

We had about 100 chickens at one point and we were gathering eggs to beat the band. One thing I remember about collecting eggs in the morning was that there weren't no civil reason to be up that early to hunt around and find where those danged birds had laid their eggs. Don't let nobody tell you elsewise, chickens are sneaky little critters which is danged amazing when you figger just how small a brain they have. They'll find the most annoying, out of the way places to lay an egg and I swear there were times that cackling was actually them laughing at us.

I remember years later, I was watching my children on an Easter egg hunt and thinking back to what those durned birds did and kind of chuckled to myself. Those kids had no idea what a real egg hunt was. Heck, I'd even found eggs up on the roof of the house one time! Crazy birds. In those days, folks did just what we did. Most folk had chickens pretty much everywhere during the day and it was a handful to keep 'em off the front porch and out of the garden. Mama kept a handful of throwing rocks in the pocket of her gardening apron to chuck at them when they decided to raid the garden. Only thing was, it just got the birds excited and more often than not, caused even more to come running into the garden to see what the ruckus was about. I reckon they figured it was Mama throwing out scraps and they sure loved her scraps. Once we decided to drop a couple of cats in the garden to chase out the chickens. Nope, chickens are pretty mean critters and they chased out the cats instead.

***

I recollect I'd mentioned about my 10th birthday some time back and the little Gordon setter Papa had brought for me from Valdosta. Well, as I'd said, I'd named him Stonewall but he was anything but that when it came to ANYTHING with feathers. I had shortened his name to Stoney as it was just easier to holler when we were out hunting or even just exploring but when he was about 6 months old I had pretty much trained him to come, sit, stay and those kinds of things. He was a natural when it came to house training him. I think we only had one "accident" when he was about 3 months old. After that he just picked up that he had to go outside to do his business.

I could hardly wait till we could get out and hunt up some quail. When he was 6 months old I got the idea to use the chickens as a training tool to get him to hold point when he saw a bird and I had actually got him to hold on point fairly well on a stray chicken wandering around. So now, more than ever, I was itching to get him out in the field in front of quail.

Well, I hate to admit it but, though it seemed like a pretty good idea at the time, it proved to be one of the worst ideas I ever came up with…though not the worst but that's another story.

I had been waiting all week to start working Stoney on pointing and all those things a good bird dog has to learn and I put my idea into practice right after breakfast one Saturday morning. I grabbed an old whistle Corine had given me for Christmas and we headed to the back of the barn where the chickens all liked to hang around. I'd no sooner rounded the corner of the barn with Stoney when one of those old Rhode Island roosters came a gliding down from the hayloft.

Now, no matter how hard those chickens flapped their wings actual flying was not on their list of accomplishments. They could swoop from one place to another if they had a high enough jumpin' off place but, 'ceptin them little banties, no real chicken that I know of could fly. We'd had a few of those little hens around but they laid such tiny eggs Papa thought 'em not worth gatherin' so he'd pretty much given up on keepin' 'em. Besides that, them danged little chickens seemed to draw hawks in like bees to honey and he'd had to kill mor'n his share of hawks over the years.

Well I watched that rooster come swooping down and 'light just behind Stony and I thought sure that dog was agonna make it to the hayloft himself. He sure hadn't been expecting no aerial attack. Stony jumped ten feet, turned around and saw that rooster standing there high and mighty and a ruffling his feathers as if to say "Gotcha". Stony just stood there for a minute and I wasn't sure what he was plannin' but he just seemed to relax a bit and then run over to me as if nothing had happened…which it hadn't… yet.

A few mornings later I'd hunted up about a dozen eggs or so and headed back to the house with Stoney following behind, never givin' me any idea he had anything on his mind but followin' me. We stepped around the corner of a fence and came face-to-beak with that rooster. Stony pretended nothing unusual was going on as he followed me on past but he let out a sudden "WOOF" and pounced on top of that rooster. He didn't damage it, just seemed satisfied with his own version of an aerial attack and he woofed again then trotted back to follow me to the house with the eggs. I'd chuckled about the display and thought he felt himself avenged.

Mama had just cooked up a batch of biscuits and we sat down for breakfast. Saturday was my one free day a week at the time, so I rushed through breakfast pretty fast. I wanted to get out and start working Stony. Hunting season was getting close and even though he was still a little young for it, I sure wanted to give him a try at hunting up quail. I grabbed my whistle and an old rope and headed out the door with Stony padding along behind me. We'd no sooner got to the far end of the barn than a hen came wandering by. Without even a woof, Stony belly-flopped on that poor old bird. Once she quit squawking, he stood up and trotted back to my side. That hen took off squawkin' and runnin' like the sky was fallin'. I scolded Stony and we headed out to the field to work on his training with the rope. As I said, he had learned to hold point on a stray chicken and had been doing pretty well but something changed in him after that morning when the rooster startled him.

We'd been out about an hour and I told Stony we had to head on back and get something to drink. It was late August and if you don't know what the weather is like in Georgia, I'm here to tell you, you can sweat out about 2 gallons of water in an hour, what with all that humidity. Stony trotted along 'side me. He was darned good about heeling. It just seemed to come natural to him. We started up the front steps and there was that danged rooster again. 'Fore I could do anything, Stony pounced. Papa saw that and hollered at the dog, then at me. I got Stony inside and Papa followed right behind. Stony hadn't hurt the bird but Papa was pretty strict about dogs that killed chickens. Stony got spanked, I got yelled at and Papa promised if that dog killed one chicken, he'd get rid of him. Well, that left me pretty shaken up and I yelled at Stony about being a bad dog. He kind of hung his head about that but didn't do much else 'ceptin' lay down next to me and go to sleep. Contrite he may have been, but he hadn't forgotten.

A couple of days later, we were heading into the barn and I'll be danged if Stony didn't pounce on another chicken. Lucky for us, Papa wasn't around. We got our egg hunting duties over with and I went back inside. Stony didn't follow me this time and I didn't give it much thought, but soon realized I was hearing a chicken squawk about every 10 minutes or so. After the third time I headed out and find out what was going on. There was Stony, over by the chicken pen standing stalk still. About a minute later an unsuspecting hen wandered by and danged if that dog didn't pounce on top of her. He wasn't trying to kill 'em but he sure enjoyed scaring the heck out of 'em. I ran over, got him by the collar and got out of there fast before Papa saw what was going on.

About a week later I told Mama the chickens seemed to have quit laying as I was finding fewer eggs every day. That's when she said she wasn't surprised. She'd seen Stony doing his pouncing act and said them birds had done got the eggs scared out of 'em. She promised to not tell Papa if I'd break Stony of his bad habit...and do it quick. It took me a couple of weeks to totally break him of hen pouncing, but I think that first day with that rooster had imprinted pretty hard on him and Stony was bound and determined that it was only fair play to get back at him.

You've heard the expression "Cock of the Walk" and that rooster shore had been but after a month of getting pounced on every couple of days that rooster started loosing his feathers and his crow. Mama caught him up one day and that was the end of him. She told Papa that rooster was getting to old to do his duty so she'd traded some crochet work for a young rooster. It wasn't no Rhode Island Red either. She said them reds were too much trouble.

Stony never bothered that young rooster and seemed content to ignore all the hens after that but it took nigh onto 2 months before them danged chickens started laying regular like. Papa licked me pretty good when I let slip about the lack of eggs. Since Stony hadn't killed any birds, he ignored his threat to get rid of him but he made him stay in the barn at night for about a week. Stony wasn't too concerned about that as the barn was full of mice and I suspect he thought it kind of a vacation. He was a great bird dog but he didn't do too bad as a mouser either.

Only frustrating thing for me was that I had to go out and catch some quail in a trap to use for training. That was a lot more work that using chickens. I tried to convince Papa that it all turned out right but I don't think ever was convinced about that. He did soften up during the next hunting season as I started bringing home a dozen or so quail every time we went out. In those days, shotgun shells were pretty dear, so you learned to not waste a shot and Stony knew where a bird went down almost every time. I don't think we lost more'n 5 birds in all the years we hunted together

Stony's pouncing solved a couple of our problems. Those chickens must've had a confab and decided to steer clear of him. Since he stretched out on the front porch much of the day, they stayed off...no more chicken droppings on the porch. He'd often go into the garden to snooze in the shade of the vegetables while Mama did her weeding...no more tearing up the soil around the new shoots.

I used a single-shot 12 gauge shotgun in those days and I reckon it worked out pretty well. I still have it and it shows its use. Today I hear about folks getting all excited about guns and I reckon they got a right to speak their minds but in all the years I hunted and even when I went over to France to fight the Kaiser, I never did see a single gun of any kind kill anything, man or beast. on it's own. A shotgun is just a tool, like any tool. Papa taught us to respect our tools, take care of 'em, and to not be careless with 'em. Maybe some folks just don't understand that.

SWAMP MONSTER
(A GOOD EXCUSE TO SHOOT)

When I was 11 or so Papa said I could go hunting with him. Finally…a chance for hunting with the grownups. I was so wound up the night before I could hardly sleep. Even so, when Papa woke me about four that morning and growled we had 10 minutes to get our britches on, eat, and get to the wagon I was up and ready. I sure didn't understand why Mel had had the temerity to sleep in his pajamas. He was what some folks call a "quick study" though because for the next few years he, too, slept in his hunting gear. Seems my getting more biscuits and bacon than he did convinced him he'd better hit the kitchen table at least close to the same time I did.

We finished in a heartbeat and were in the wagon ready to go 'fore Papa had finished his coffee. We sat there waiting in the cold, fearful of being left at home if we got out.

Papa had harnessed up the horse 'fore he called us so we started out about quarter to five. It wasn't a long trip down to the swamp but Papa said it was better to take the wagon in case we did get a deer. The wagon would save us a long walk back to the house and besides, he wasn't too keen on walking around in the swamp with moccasins waiting to snuggle up and say "Hello".

Trust me when I say I didn't want no part of talking to a moccasin either unless with the talking end of a gun. This was back in the day when plain folks couldn't afford good snake boots. Now don't get confused. Snake boots ain't what they sound like. They're not made of snakes' skins but of thick cow or buffalo hide—thick enough snake fangs can't penetrate 'em. Snake boot promoters'll tell you a snake will only strike a body below the knee. I never was sure anyone had ever told a snake that was the rule. Later on I reckoned even if the snake had read the rule it was better to have some protection than none at all.

Papa and Uncle Earl had built some deer stands down on Cat Creek a few years before and 'fore the start of hunting season they'd go out and nail new burlap around the top of the stand as a cover to conceal movement.

They had rigged up a bench that folded up against one side of the stand if no one was up there. A few years later they figured putting in a chair that swiveled around would work better. You could then turn all the way around without getting a crick in your neck and some sneaky deer, bear, or monster couldn't creep up behind a body. At this time though a feller just had to sit on the bench. It wasn't too bad for the first 15 minutes but after that, it got harder and harder.

Down about 200 yards or so from Cat Creek they'd built a tower stand. The floor was about 12 feet off the ground. Mel and I had helped nail all the burlap around a few weeks before. Papa walked with me down to the stand and waited while I shinnied up the thing. He handed my 12-gauge up to me and told me to stay put 'til he come for me. I was 11 years old and a little feller, and had no desire to go wandering around in a swamp in the dark no how. So his warning to stay put could have stayed down inside him as far as I was concerned.

The swamps were full of bear, panther, moccasins, rattlesnakes, coral snakes and, of course, the feared skunk ape. Well, that's what we called those critters. A skunk ape was what folks out west called a Sasquatch or Big Foot. Ain't sure where the name Sasquatch came from but Big Foot was supposed to be because they were giant hairy things and would sneak up on a body and grab 'em. Well, all of you fellers remember as an 11 year-old boy having a pretty darned good imagination. I hunkered down in my oversized coat and I could hear Papa a slipping back up to the wagon to get Mel. He hadn't been gone long when I realized just how quiet—or noisy—it is in the swamp. I heard a train whistle way off and was rather surprised by that as the closest railroad tracks were clean over in Hahira and that was most 15 miles away as the horse walked. Thinking on it, I reckoned it wasn't near as far as all that if you could go straight, which of course a body wouldn't and probably couldn't so that was of no never mind.

Through the dark I could see a light spot off 'mongst the trees that was considering letting the sun shine in pretty soon. It's funny how you can sit in a stand and everything be so quiet. And quick as all that you start hearing things. Every little thing. Something hit the ground and I knowed it was that skunk ape a coming for me. I could swear I heard footsteps. I was determined no skunk ape was gonna carry me off. I kept my eyes as wide open as I could and my shotgun handy. The irony was that, as wide-awake and watchful as I was, I started getting sleepy. I'd scooted around so's to get as comfortable as a body can get on a hard, narrow wooden bench. And while I'd never believed the stories of hunters taking a nap while sitting out in the woods, shivering with cold (or fear) and feeding skeeters, I was nigh on to letting it happen to me! I'd 'bout stretched myself into the least uncomfortable position I could get and was nigh on to falln' asleep, when I heered this low mmmaaaaahhhh sound. I ignored it the first time, thinking it was just my imagination or maybe that it was just the way I was sitting with my hat mushed up against my ear. I sure heard it the second time though and I sat up and started looking round to see what was coming for me. Meeeaaaaaahhhh it sounded again, only this time it was closer and it was coming my way.

Well Ol' Sol hisself was a sneaking over the horizon and I could see a bit better now. Only thing was, half-dark is way more scary than black-dark. Boy-oh-boy does your imagination really start a going. I'd thought it bad when I couldn't see nothing but shades of black. Now I could see a bit more.

I spotted a squirrel hoping around, picking up an acorn, running off a bit then coming back to look for more. I say "hoping" around 'cause when you're watching them you get a feeling they was just hoping to find something. I have to tell you, I've heard all kinds of stories about how squirrels store up nuts and things for winter but after watching them I can tell you, they ain't got the slightest idea where they put something and they run around a digging here and there and probably thinking "where the heck is all my food?"

Watching the squirrel had made me forget about that monster for a moment but about then it come a moaning even closer. I was all set to figure a way to climb up even higher in a nearby oak tree but I had to put that idea out of mind. It would have required my climbing down off that stand and I knew I'd be got 'fore I could get to the oak. I'd just have to make my stand right here.

I didn't have but two shells of buck shot but if it was grabbin' for me, I'd put that 12-gauge right in its face and blast it with both barrels. Assuming I hadn't fainted first.

Meeeeaaaaahhh... It was comin' at me from behind. I peered out and saw some movement. I squirmed around to get in position to stop it climbing the tree. Then she slipped around a clump of fennel weeds and again cried Meeeeaaaaahhh. I just knelt there with my mouth hanging open. It was a big old doe and she were bleating like I watched a goat do a few times over at a neighbor's farm. She had a tongue that musta stuck out a foot and she was bleating for her fawn I reckon. I danged near shot her just for scaring me so bad. She walked right past the stand bleating about every 15 or 20 feet and slowly vanished into the brush. I heard her till well past sunup but at least I knowed what it was and I finally did doze off for a while.

I never saw another deer that morning but after my ordeal with what I was sure was the dreaded skunk ape I didn't care to see one anyway. I saw a family of 'coons go scampering through and, of course, the normal bounty of squirrels and birds and even a big old owl.

If you've never had an owl fly close by you've missed out on a mystery of nature. That owl couldn't have been more that five feet from me when he went by but I didn't hear even a whisper of wind. You can hear the wings and wind of other birds but there's something in how God put owls together to make em deadly silent. I heard of some folks shooting and even eating owls but I could never understand why. Seems to me, they're a special kind of critter and worth watching. They sure are a wonder.

I've sat many a deer stand since that morning and have seen a lot of things go wandering by. Down in Florida many years later I was sitting on a stand and heard the most awful racket and remembered the skunk ape. The brush-tearing turned to grunting so I bravely peeked over the edge. It was only a black bear ripping up a palm to get at the meat inside. Folks call that swamp cabbage. I've eaten it but didn't reckon it was good enough to warrant all that work. Guess the bears like it though.

Nowadays there's folks who complain about hunters and taking game animals for food. I reckon they got a right to fuss if they want to. For me, I know the Lord gave us dominion over all the creatures and I believe that's what was intended. I think hunting makes a body slow down and gives him time to consider things more carefully. It gives the soul a bit of rest as well, to my way of thinking. I reckon I had some of the most sincere conversations with the Lord sitting out in the woods. Sometimes though, I have to admit, there were times I was asking Him why he made so danged many skeeters! Maybe He figgered that was nature's way of getting even.

I've met a lot of folks out in the woods over the years. Some of the best folks I ever knew and many who became lifelong friends are those I met while out in the woods. I think it's 'cause we all had a desire to get back to a simple way of being. Just a body listening to what one feller said was the call of the wild.

Speaking of that, my dog is telling me he's got a calling, so I'll sign off for now and let you folks get back to doing whatever you were doing 'fore I interrupted you.

ELLEN

BAM! "You got 'im Mel!" I hollered at the report of the shotgun and we watched the duck come spiraling down.

"Go get it Stoney", I told my dog. Stoney just sat there watching as the duck went crashing into the little pond we were on; rather we were standing beside. I told him again to go fetch the bird. Stoney just looked up at me and backed out of the little blind a bit further. At first I thought he was going to just slip out and around. Only he didn't. Oh, he slipped out alright but around apparently wasn't part of his game plan. He padded on over to a little grassy patch underneath a live oak and plopped down. I hollered at him till I was blue but he just lay there.

Mel came over and said, "Well Herm, I reckon that answers that about your amazing dog. He ain't no retriever".

"The heck he ain't. You watch. I'll get him on that duck in a couple of minutes." Well, I did everything but throw that dog in the pond but he just wouldn't have a thing to do with going after that duck. Mel, being the kind and loving brother he was just sat there snickering about the whole deal and pretty soon, here comes another flock.

...BAM, BAM...one miss, one down. The wounded bird whirled over like an airplane and kind of glided down. Only this time it hit the edge of the cornfield we were in, next to the pond. I didn't even get a chance to holler for Stoney. I saw him bee-lining his way to the bird. He ran over, picked it up and came trotting back to me as happy as you please. Turned out, he didn't object to retrieving, he just objected to getting into cold water when there was a pretty heavy hoar frost on the ground. Seems that dog was a whole lot smarter than I was! I apologized to him and promised I'd make sure I shot ducks over warm water or dry land from then on. I doubt he understood what I said but I kept that promise. I retrieved the first duck after almost dunking myself reaching for it with a long branch. Stoney just sat and watched, apparently content to stay dry.

Describing how that bird glided down like an airplane is kind of amusing to me now. That hunt was years before we ever even saw an aeroplane, airplane in today's lingo, so it's not a term I'd have even known back then. I reckon at that time, there weren't mor'n a dozen of 'em at most as it was well before the Great War, as we called it later, and what they called flying wouldn't have been considered soaring either!

Mel and I loved to bird hunt together but most often my hunts consisted of just me and Stoney. Mel was a kind of a ladies man; at least he thought he was. He may have been younger than I was but he was always more interested in the fairer sex. Not to say I wasn't interested but most of the gals my age were just not appealing to me. I'd seen a couple gals over in Ray City I'd a'been interested in but they may as well have been in Atlanta for all that. Ray City was a good 15 miles away and we were years before having an automobile and besides, I was only around 13 or so at the time. We had an aunt who lived out on the west end of Ray City but our visits to her were limited to a couple of times a year.

That particular hunt was on a Saturday morning and more of a rare treat than normal. Living on a farm meant working most every day except for Sundays and even then there were times that we had to work in the afternoon. Sunday mornings though were always reserved for church. No matter what. I think I wrote about us being Methodists but the only church we had in the area was the Primitive Baptist church a couple miles down the road in Cat Creek. I'd once seen Mama roll her eyes at the church ladies down there but Mama was too strict in her upbringing to ever let them see her do that. But I saw and I was stunned. I'd never seen her be that judgmental of anyone.

There was a change one particular Sunday morning. In attendance were the family that had bought the old Lee farm down the road a ways. Sitting between her parents was a gal with reddish blonde hair…the prettiest gal I'd ever seen. I couldn't stop staring. She looked us over early on and I must have scared her 'cause she quickly looked away and didn't look back my way during the rest of the service.

***

In those days the church always had a kind of social after the service. Those who could brought something to share with others for dinner. That would be lunch in today's language. Supper in those days was nighttime eating. Mama most always brought fried chicken or, on occasions, a pecan or peach pie. But that day she'd fried up a mess of venison steaks for breakfast and had made extra to bring to the social. It was from a deer Mel and I managed to get a couple of weeks earlier so we figured it was fine to share as we had plenty in the cooler.

There were several tables underneath some pecan trees out back of the church and all the food was laid out for everyone to get whatever they were of a mind to eat. The new family brought some peach cobbler, which anyone who knows me knows it's my favorite dessert. As people were milling around picking some of this and that, the little redheaded girl came over and looking at what Mama had put out and asked if she might have a piece of beef steak.

"Ain't no beef steaks. It's venison," I said to her.

"What's venison"? she asked.

"What's vension? Haven't you ever had venison before? It's deer meat".

"A dear what"? she asked.

"A deer. A white tail deer. Haven't you ever seen deer before"?

"I don't think so. We just moved here from Chicago. Father was tired of living in the city and he wanted to get back to how he grew up, which was on a farm. The only animals I ever saw were horses and of course cows and hogs. I saw some sheep one time though. Funny little things and they sound funny too"

Well, you can imagine my surprise at all that. I couldn't imagine anyone not knowing what deer were. She took two pieces of venison and went back to sit with her parents. Mel sat down and I saw he had what looked to be half a plate of peach cobbler. I just shook my head. Mel had one other love besides girls and that was food. Peach cobbler was his favorite dessert too. I had to force him to stop eating long enough to tell me where he got it. He finally mumbled that the new folks brought it. I grabbed a plate and half a dozen pieces of venison and headed over to the new folks table.

"Like it?" I asked.

"Oh yes I've never had anything like it before. I was telling Mother and Father about where we could get some and Father was just explaining to me about hunting for deer when he was a boy but I guess it won't be so easy now."

"Lots easier than you think…here." With that, I put the plate of steaks on the table and said we had a lot of meat for the next few weeks and they were welcome to it and that if they wanted, I'd even bring some over.

Her name was Ellen Jensen. When she introduced me to her parents her father said he was grateful for the chance to enjoy venison again after so many years away. He confirmed what Ellen had said; that he had been raised on a farm but up in Kansas. Years of life in the big city had worn on him and he was determined to get back to farming.

"Son, any time you feel you have too much venison, don't be shy to let us know! I'll not be too proud to relieve you of some and hope to find myself in the woods come winter. I'd even pay you for the meat".

I pointed out it was illegal to sell game meat but I promised to bring them a gift of some venison the next day after school if I could get all my chores done in time. Ellen offered more cobbler and I wasn't too shy about accepting it either!

Mr. Jensen said he was a lawyer and while he'd made good money up in Chicago, he'd just had enough of big city living. He spoke a lot of high dollar words I didn't really understand but the gist of it was he just wanted to get away. Said he'd cashed out his share of the firm he was with and headed south to get back to what he called a "normal" life.

I saw Ellen the next morning in school and there had been quite a discussion on what grade she should be in. The teacher wanted to put her in the 10th grade because of her level of education. But then, because of her age they could put her in the 9th. Well dang, I was only in the 8th. Seems those big city schools did a lot more educating than ours did. Anyway, Mrs. Bozeman said she'd write to her old school for her records and figure it out then. That may seem normal now in the bigger schools today but we were all in the same classroom. All told there weren't but about 20 of us in the school and nearly half of 'em was us! I introduced Ellen to everyone at lunchtime that day and we sat and talked about all things youngsters talked about in those days. I asked a lot of questions about Chicago and she told me how big the city was, which I was doubtful of at the time but found out years later that she'd likely been kind of conservative on things. I told her about Mel and me shooting the deer and how it took us a good part of the morning just to get it back to the house. She asked how big a deer was. Without thinking, I said it was about three or four times as big as Stoney. Then she warmed my heart…she asked who, or what, Stoney was.

"Stoney is my bird dog. Papa brought him home for me a couple of years ago as a pup." I told her he was a Gordon Setter and how good a bird dog he was, only don't ever ask him to jump in a pond of cold water for anything. Ellen got kind of quiet then and finally asked me if I could teach her how to hunt. Well, I liked to have choked on a piece of carrot I'd just stuck in my mouth. Teach a GIRL to hunt? Girls hunt? Girls? With a gun? I just looked at her after I'd quit choking and asked if she was serious. I said ain't no girls around here that hunt that I knew of. She got kind of red in the face but not because she was embarrassed but mad. Said she'd already asked her father for a gun for her birthday and she'd find someone else to teach her who wasn't a snob. At that, she got up and just left me sitting there, still trying to keep that carrot down.

I chewed on that conversation and I think that carrot, for a long time. I was still thinking about it when I got home from school. I waited until after supper that evening and finally when we were all sitting in the parlor I asked Papa about girls hunting and had he ever heard of anything as crazy.

"Well son, I'll tell you. I met your mother when I wasn't a whole lot older than you are now. Well, maybe a bit more than that but the point is she'd never hunted or fished neither and like you I purely loved doing both. Because I loved it, she joined in as well. I taught her to hunt and fish and if you were around back then and looking for one of us, you'd as likely find both of us, either in the woods or in a boat."

"MAMA! You hunted?" I asked in astonishment.

"And did my share of fishing too! How do you think I knew how to cook all those fish and birds you boys bring home? Your Papa and I did a lot of both long before any of you children ever came along. I finally had to quit as all of you are more than enough to be hunting up now. As much as I love your Papa and being outdoors I love you children more so. Some day, maybe after all of you are gone and out of our hair, I'll get back to it. For now, it's fine that I do my hunting in the kitchen keeping all of you fed and clothed and out of trouble. Speaking of clothed, you bust another hole in your shirt I just made for you and you might have a chilly time this winter wearing nothing but britches in school! Lord only knows how you manage to tear your clothes so!"

Needless to say, that was quite a revelation to all of us. Mama hunted! Made a body wonder at things one never would have even considered. Parents can sure fool a person.

Next morning I got to school even earlier than I normally did as I wanted to catch Ellen before it started. Well, she didn't show up that day or the next day either. I got to wondering if they had left or if someone was sick. When she didn't show the third day, I determined I'd go over after school. Half an hour after school was out I was knocking at their door. Mrs. Jensen opened the door and said I had to stay outside as Ellen had been very sick with the Whooping Cough. Said she was out of danger now but that it would a while before she'd be able to go out and that they weren't taking any chances on spreading it to anyone else. I left, sorry she'd been sick but relieved to hear she was mending.

It was better'n a week 'fore she came to school and while she was still kind of pale looking, the doctor had told her she was no longer contagious and was well enough to go to school.

I was chomping at the bit all morning to talk to her and when lunchtime finally came, I made a point of telling Ellen I'd be proud to teach her to hunt and to fish if she was of a mind to do that as well. I told her it would cost her though. When she demanded to know what the cost was, I told her one big mess of peach cobbler! There was a momentary look of confusion and then delight when she heard what the cost was.

I did teach her to hunt, how to dress birds out and finally one day, late that winter, how to dress a deer. Ellen had been given her birthday present. A brand new 16 gauge double barrel and one I'd have almost given up peach cobbler for…almost. She gave me a run for my money on doves but I'd usually win out on quail.

Her daddy's plan to become a farmer again never really did pan out. They worked the farm hard for a couple of years but about halfway through the third year, sold the farm and moved to Tallahassee down in Florida. I read sometime later that he'd gone into politics and was working for the government down there. I eventually lost touch with Ellen but I'll never forget those couple of years. Mel kept trying to court her at first but Ellen was my girl, my first girl. She kissed me that day she shot her first deer…on the mouth too!

I never did tell Ethylene about her. Some things you just don't tell you wife, especially if it was about your first love.

PAPA'S SECOND MISTAKE

One morning just before my 13th birthday I watched Papa head out in the wagon. Mama said he was going over to Hahira to pick up a pair of mules he wanted to use for dragging in some pine logs he and Uncle Jake had cut down a few months before. They were intent on opening up another field down towards Cat Creek so Papa wanted to get the trees dragged out and the stumps removed that winter so he'd have an extra few acres for cotton come spring. Only thing was, our two horses were buggy horses and not strong enough to do log and stump pulling.

I'd heard Uncle Jake a couple of nights before talking about getting some oxen but oxen were getting kind of scarce in those days. Uncle Jake had reckoned what they needed to do was get a couple of mules to do the work instead. He'd reasoned a mule ain't no bigger'n a horse but they tend to have a lot more strength and more of a one track mind. Once you got 'em going on something, they worked right on. Papa said he'd sleep on the idea and let him know the next day.

About 8 o'clock that night, the telephone rang. It was Uncle Jake asking Papa what he'd decided on. Uncle Jake had made a few phone calls and had located a pair of mules over in Hahira. The feller wanted 25 dollars apiece but if Papa wanted 'em and came and got 'em the next morning, he would sell 'em both for 35 dollars. Papa agreed to that…said he'd pick up Uncle Jake in the morning and they'd go over together to get the mules. Papa groused about the 35 dollars. It was a whole lot of money and he only needed them for the winter. But it might be worth it to have a pair that would do the work and he'd sell 'em in the spring.

I'd heard 'im talking about getting the logs stacked up back of the barn. He had a buyer lined up who'd haul 'em on down to the lumber mill in Valdosta. Offered Papa a nickel a foot for good pine, which was pretty good money in those days. Add that to the newly cleared land and Papa said we'd be in high cotton the next year.

High cotton, case you didn't know was the kind of cotton you didn't have to bend over to pick. It was easy to get to. I'd known about that for a long time and I'm here to tell you, there's high cotton and then there's higher cotton as far as I was concerned. For one thing, in them days I was kind of a little feller and I didn't come up to bout half as tall as my Papa. High cotton for him was about a foot too high for me. It was my beginnings of understanding the theory of relativity. If you're a short feller like I was, anything above the kitchen sink was relatively tough to get to and the opposite can be said for anything down low like the lower kitchen cabinets or hunting for chicken eggs. A little feller didn't have near the problems getting chicken eggs like a tall character might. I also didn't get picked on for fighting in school near as often as the bigger kids did either. So, depending on how you looked at it, there were advantages and disadvantages to both.

Well, the day came on bright and clear and cold enough to darn near freeze the creek. There was so much hoar frost around you could almost skate on it. Looked pretty but after a half hour in the barn picking up eggs, I was cold enough to snap in two myself and all I wanted was to get inside and spend some warming-up time thinking about how to get the big buck I had seen the week before. I thought about going hunting soon as I'd thawed some but I figured it just wasn't worth it that morning. Any sensible deer, or even a quail, would be curled up tight under a pine tree burrowed in the needles.

Funny thing about cold weather in the south…most Yankee folks I've met, and I hear tell folks out west, think it don't get cold down here. They ain't tried to sit still on a deer stand or in a duck blind when it's below thirty in our kind of cold. When I was over in France a few years later, I heard someone complaining about how cold it was and I just kind of smiled. See, we had to sit pretty danged still there too but it weren't the same as that ol' down-south cold I grew up with. But at least our ol' Georgia deer couldn't shoot back! But I digress.

Papa had loaded up some things Mama wanted him to take to her sister over in Hahira since he was heading that way anyway. Some of it was some sewing things Mama had been working on for sewing up a couple of quilts. Mama would get 'em started and then send what she'd done over to Aunt Caroline to finish. They'd do that all winter and come the spring fair the next year, they'd sell 'em off and start new ones.

Anyway, Papa got loaded up and headed out early for Uncle Jake's and then Hahira. He'd left a note to not expect him until supper at the earliest and if he was to be later, he'd stay on over at Uncle Jakes place til morning. Uncle Jake only lived about a mile and a half or so away but nighttime in Georgia, particularly in the winter, wasn't no time to be out on the road.

Nights are so dark you couldn't see a ghost…if you was inclined to be looking for one. Besides, with it being so darned cold, it wasn't a good idea to be wandering around in the dark anyway. Near the only good thing of being so cold in the dark was you didn't have to worry about snakes like you did of a summer night.

Well, around three o'clock that afternoon the telephone rang. It was 2 short bursts and a long ring. We had what they used to call a party line. Each farm had a trunk line that went out to the main line out of the sub-station. If you was wanting to phone someone who wasn't on your line you had to ring the operator and she (it was always a "she") would have to put you through. Each house had a special ring so's you'd know it was for you. Ours was 2 shorts and a long.

With all the neighbors being on the same line I can tell you it was the fastest gossipy thing I think anyone ever created. If the phone rang anyone on that line could pick up their extension and eaves drop on what was happening. You learned early on to be particular on what you said. We once had a neighbor who not only listened but felt compelled to comment at inopportune times about what she'd heard. Papa, in a phone conversation with Uncle Jake said to watch what he said 'cause we had a big-eared ol' cow down the road who needed to be corralled someplace without a telephone for a while. In a matter of hours, her husband come over and asked what for he was saying bad things about his sweet wife. Papa, not too gently, explained about eaves-droppers hearing only bad things about themselves. Don't know if that stopped the listening in but it sure stopped the blabber-mouth holding forth at community events…within Papa's hearing at any rate.

Mama answered the phone and it was Papa saying he'd be later than he reckoned. Said he was having some issues with the mules and it'd be best for them to stay over at Caroline's house in Hahira. Mama said to give her love to Caroline and that if he needed anything to just ring back in the morning and she'd send the boys.

If you'd known my Papa you'd know he didn't hardly ever ask for help, so we didn't think more about it. Mama did remind us that Papa not being there didn't mean we could skip out on our chores. We knew that and knew her reminding us was a warning to not be trying to sneak off 'fore our chores were done…as if we would. Only thing was, we'd done 'em already so I asked Mama if I could slip out and go on down to see if I could catch that buck I'd been seeing down the road where the creek and the road crossed.

She just looked at me, nodded and 'fore she could think up a reason to stop me I'd grabbed my shotgun from behind the kitchen door and was halfway to the barn when I heard her holler to not be out beyond dark. My shotgun was what they called a Remington Rider Single Barrel and had been around for a bit 'fore I got mine. I'd saved up for three years for it and it was my first new gun…one I'd researched and read about and saved for and bought myself. I sure loved that gun. It wasn't one of those fancy rifle guns but just a simple shotgun that did its job. Down our way you didn't need more'n that if you knew what you were doing. Turns out, that shotgun got us many a bird and buck over the next few years. It's a collectors' item now and I've heard my grandson has it hanging on his wall. I reckon that's probably a safe place for it…it's earned it's retirement.

My older brother Fred and I had built a little platform about 15 feet up in an old live oak just above a deer trail. We'd only been able to sit it a couple of times. We had school now and it was mighty hard to get home, get our chores done and still have time to get to a stand before dark and stay there till darkness set in…knowing you don't leave your stand while it's still daylight.

I was at that tree in less than 20 minutes. I'd put my shotgun up against the tree and tied the rope around it to haul it up. Once I had climbed the tree and pulled my gun up I loaded it with a 12 gauge double-ought buck shell and put the extra one on a flatish branch next to me. One rule I never had to be told was to only load your gun when you were ready to shoot it. I don't recall anybody ever telling me that, just seemed logical. Never could understand trying to save time by loading early.

I got myself settled down and by then it was close to 4:30 and I was glad I'd had a chance to get there and let all my scrambling around quiet down. About 45 minutes later I heard some rustling and looked over across the creek. It was just a skunk sneaking around trying to find it's supper. I thought to be grateful skunks can't climb trees then wondered if they could. It was starting to get on to dark and I knew I didn't have much more time fore' I'd have to shinny down and get on home. I'd seen a couple of does meander into the field across the road but they was just a grazing around and didn't seem bothered by nothing. It weren't five minutes later I saw them does start a running towards the road and bolt across as if a cougar was after 'em. Then I saw that buck. I reckoned he'd been watching those gals too.

He came out of the woods on the other side of the road not forty feet from me and was heading my way with his head down and snorting at the ground. I waited until he was almost under the tree but then saw I wasn't going to have a shot, even as close as he was, unless he raised his head. I reckon I didn't even think about it as I whistled. He stopped and looked up. I fired with him not more'n 15 feet away. Then I heard the shout.

Following the shout was the sound of a wagon on the road and horses going crazy. It was Papa and Uncle Jake heading home. That durned deer had turned around and headed back towards the field only to drop dead right in front of them. Those mules stood up on their hind legs, let out a scream that convinced me they were not horses and took off with Papa hanging on for dear life and hollering in a peculiar foreign language If you know what I mean.

Papa had fashioned a lantern on the front of the wagon to see by and from my view point, all I could see was the shadow of those runaway critters and that lantern swinging back and forth, all a going down the road like they was heading to freedom. It was only about a mile and a half to the house and Papa managed to get those mules stopped by the time he got to Cat Creek Road. I knew there wasn't nothing I could do to help him so I went up and pulled the deer off the road then began dressing it out, all the while trying to figure when my funeral was going to be.

Papa came riding back up the road on one of the team horses. He'd had them tied to the back of the wagon and they'd managed to keep up with those crazy mules. He'd left the mules with Uncle Jake and came back to find me.

Papa never said a word. He just got down and helped me finish dressing out that buck and drape it over the horse, along with me. All the way back the house he stayed silent and I was even more sure my funeral would be the next day...or that I would wish it was.

I slide off the horse and helped Papa hang the deer just inside the barn for the night then he told me to go inside and get cleaned up and he'd be in directly. I went in, washed up, changed my clothes, and was sitting at the kitchen table when he walked in. He washed his hands and poured himself a cup of coffee from the old pot that always sat on the warming rack. Then Uncle Jake came in from taking care of the mules, the wagon, and the horses and did the same thing.

Papa sat down on the other side of the table and looked over at Uncle Jake and said, "You know Jake, buying them danged mules was only the second mistake of my life." Uncle Jake just looked at him and finally asked him what his first mistake was. Papa, just kind of grinned, looked at me and said, "Having children...nice shot son." With that he got up and said he was tired and going to bed. No funeral?

The next morning we finished butchering the deer. Papa allowed it was one of the nicest bucks he'd ever seen taken. It was a nice eating deer, too. It had almost an inch of fat on it's back from feeding on the corn in the area. I've shot a few more deer over the years but he was my first and finest. Also the most tender venison we ever had.

About a week later Uncle Jake, after swearing me to secrecy, told me Papa had been telling his friends the story of that night. Papa didn't tell me, of course, but he was taking on some of the blame for the whole uproar 'cause he was the one who'd altered his plans.

He'd changed his mind about staying in Hahira, thinking the lantern would shed enough light if they just took their time. That way they could surprise Mama and get an early start on the logs the next morning. He had forgot about that deer stand right near the creek crossing and didn't take into account just how plain crazy about hunting I was. He also hadn't allowed for the event of a dying deer landing on the road right in front of skittish mules and really how ornery they could be when they were a mind to be...which turned out to be oftener than he knew.

Papa was so surprised and pleased he just didn't have the heart to punish me for doing what come natural to me. Uncle Jake told me Papa was sure proud of how I got that deer and said he sure wished he could have had a photographer come take a picture of me with it. But cameras and photographers were a luxury and the picture in our minds is still there, as fresh as any photograph would ever be. As for me, this is the first time I ever told about that night. I reckon after 50 years, Papa will forgive me for telling it.

They got the logs skidded up and the stumps cleared before Christmas and Papa said the best Christmas present he could think of was selling those mules to the first Yankee that came by. On 'tother hand he didn't think so harsh on the Yankees he'd do a thing like that to an unsuspecting feller, no matter his religion. As it turned out, the lumber mill fella said he could use a couple of mules and gave Papa 50 dollars for the pair, so it turned out even better. Papa had them for two months or so and sold them for a profit while making a profit for the farm. He never did try to use mules again. Said he'd sooner stick his head in a hole down on the creek to check out the moccasin population than ever own another mule.

He got almost 300 dollars for the timber and I know he shared that with Uncle Jake. Bringing in that kind of money for a farmer in the middle of winter was a pretty rare thing so that was the best Christmas we ever had. Everyone got something extra special. Mama finally got a real sewing machine. It took her about week and a lot of needle holes in her fingers 'fore she got used to it but she sure put it to use after that.

Papa paid a fella from down in Valdosta to come up and take a picture of my deer antlers and me. I've still got it. Cost almost 5 dollars. I also got a new Sunday suit as well as a grand skinning knife. I gave that knife to my son on his 13th birthday many years later. It had a bit of wearing down on it by then but it was the best skinning knife I ever owned.

THE BEAR AND A GIRL'S SCREAM

Word had gone 'round there was a bear wandering the woods between us and Cat Creek Primitive Baptist Church. That got us all pretty excited 'cause in those days you'd see sign of bear once in a while but they weren't all that common near an active farm. There was a fair amount of farms in the area, all hives of activity and all with a passel of dogs so bears just tended to avoid the area. That fall though, there'd been not just bear sign but a couple of sightings as well. So we accepted it as more than idle talk. No one had lost any livestock yet but folks were figuring if that bear stayed around much longer it might be only a matter of time before it decided taking down a young calf would be a whole lot less work than trying to catch something wild like a deer.

Papa had talked to a feller over to Ray City who reckoned it must be young as the tracks they'd been seein' weren't overly large and the scat they'd found seemed to indicate a small critter, too. Now if you've ever seen bear scat from a big ol' boar, you'd know what I mean. Bears are funny critters and not too particular where they squat to do what comes natural. More often than not you'll find that "reject" pile right in the middle of the trail or anywhere in a field they happen to be wandering through

Bill Walton was a kid about my age at the time. His folks had moved down from Tennessee a couple years before and while we had bummed around a bit, I'd never done any serious hunting with him. I'd taken him out to shoot some birds with me an' Stony but he didn't seem all that interested in bird hunting. But when he heard about the bear, his eyes lit up like he'd just seen President Roosevelt or something extra special like a girl with bare legs…which was a whole lot different than seeing a bear leg.

Bill came running up the road one morning all excited and said he just had to talk to me alone. Papa seemed to know the signs. Said if I was planning on doin' anything in the afternoon, I'd best be getting all my chores done first. Only thing was, he know'd I'd already done my chores. But young Bill was always running. Papa reckoned he had two speeds…high gear and overdrive and I think Papa wanted to add some lead to Bill's britches in hopes of slowin' him down a bit.

Bill started apesterin' me to hurry up and get my chores done as he had some powerful news. He figured we had to get going if'n we were to have any kind of luck. I stopped him there and said, "Bill, we're always gonna have some kind of luck and I, fer one, want it to be the good kind 'cause the other kind just ain't no kind of fun". He frowned at me and said "Huh?"

I shook my head, said, "Never mind," then asked what was so all fired important that we had to rush off. He told me he'd run across bear scat down by Cat Creek just north of the church and that it was still fresh and that if we hurried down we might be able to catch that bear and beat out all those old men, meaning my Papa and his friends, who'd been trying for a week to catch that ol' bear. That decided it for me. The prospect of shooting a bear was one I'd never before entertained. Assurin' him I'd just that moment finished my chores, I grabbed up my shotgun and buckshot and we headed out.

We wasted no time getting down to the creek where Bill had seen the scat and from there we started off slowly, stalking the tracks as best we could. Now if you've ever tried to follow bear tracks through the woods, you know it's a heck of a challenge. First off, bears have soft feet and unless they step in some bare dirt or a patch of mud, it's not easy to see which way they may be going. There were several times we lost him but then we'd get on to where he'd left a couple of marks where his claws had dug into the ground and we kept on searching. We'd left the farm about 3 that afternoon and hadn't given any thought to it coming on dark so neither of us had a lantern or even matches for making a torch out of cattails which, in and of itself, is a challenge. Along about five, I realized we'd never make it back to the house before dark so we gave up on the bear and started heading back. We'd no more'n changed directions when we heard something in the brush. I whispered to Bill to get to the other side of the trail and slip on around through the woods and see if he couldn't nudge that bear out for me to get a shot at. Bill was rather disinclined to go busting through brush with a bear in the neighborhood without any means of defending himself and it took a bit of cajoling to convince him I'd be between him and the bear…at least that's what I told him, though I had my own doubts as to how accurate that statement was.

Bill slipped off to the right and I could hear him like he was a tractor going through the brush. I ain't sure if he was making all that racket to discourage the bear or just cause he didn't understand the idea of slipping through the woods. As it turned out I reckon it didn't matter much 'cause the sound of leaves and such crackling had stopped. When it started up again the sounds were heading my way! Well, I'll tell ya' that didn't give me much comfort either and I'm the one what had the shotgun!

Then, I'll be danged if that bear didn't materialize right in the middle of a clear patch amid the brush not more'n 30 feet from me and I had a good shot at him. I laid him a hard one and he took off like the wind. I knew I'd hit him but buckshot ain't the most penetrating projectiles and I only had that single shot. I never got a chance to put another shell in before he was gone.

Bill came tearing out of the brush and hollering at me and swearing the bear almost ran over him. I knew that wasn't likely as Bill had been on the other side of the trail. We walked on over to where it'd been standing and we could see a bit of blood on the ground. We started tracking the blood trail but my saner side took over and I told Bill under no circumstances was I going to keep tracking a wounded bear in the dark. If the bear had been hit hard he couldn't go far. The smart thing for us to do was head for home then head out early in the morning to track him.

Back at the farm, Bill phoned his folks for permission to spend the night explaining we'd shot the bear and wanted to go early in the morning to find it. Then we spent our supper telling my folks what had happened. Mama wasn't too pleased about our going after the bear but Papa just kind of chuckled; said he was a bit surprised we'd found it but was glad we'd done the right thing by backing out when the sun started going down. He offered to help us go out come mornin' and we all headed off to bed.

I woke at dawn to the smell of ham and eggs. Busy over the stove, Papa said he wanted to get an early start and saw no reason to get Mama up to cook for a couple of crazy kids. I kind of suspect that "crazy" was meant for himself as well. Breakfast was served and gone just about quicker than it took to tell and we loaded up the wagon and headed on down to where we'd last seen the bear.

Papa left the wagon about half a mile away as even a deer would have had trouble navigating the trail we'd used the night before. I'd made a pile of branches to mark where I'd been and once there Bill and I headed on into the woods. Papa said he'd stay on the trail and follow along as best he could. I'd grabbed some rope and rigged up a kind of backpack the night before thinking we'd just tie up the bear and walk out with it on our backs.

The beginning of our tracking started off pretty easy as there was a fair amount of blood trail to follow but it kept getting thinner and thinner and my hopes were growing thinner as well. We'd followed him right along in spite of the diminishing evidence and saw where he'd hit a little dribbled up kind of creek that sometimes flowed on into Cat Creek. From there the tracks were more evident but then they disappeared altogether. When we came to a fair sized briar patch I warned Bill if that bear had burrowed into those briars we'd pay the devil getting it out of there. I thought to sneak round to the other side of the patch hoping to find a point where I could see further into it.

I'd just reached the other side when all of the sudden I heard a girl screaming her head off…loud and long enough to wake all those folks over at the cemetery. It sure woke me up! I went running back around the patch and there stood Bill, still hollering. Though he didn't sound like a girl any more he was sure agitated.

"You found him" I said and he proceeded to use some of those words we'd only ever heard from Papa. He was shouting something about him not finding the bear but the bear finding him. Papa's showing up had a calming effect and Bill was able to tell us what happened. He'd been slipping up against the briar patch peering in as best he could when he happened to glance down and that bear was laying there with one paw stretched out and almost touching his foot. He thought the bear had reached out to grab him and that's when he screamed. Papa and I were teasing him about screaming all the while he kept saying he'd like to know how I'd have reacted seeing that bear's paw right at my foot. I reckon he's right about that as I'd been a bit surprised as well.

We decided to not try to dress the bear out there but to carry him out whole and do all that business when we got back to the wagon. The bear was probably only a 3-year old and was only around 140 pounds or so. After taking turns carrying him out, we all swore, Papa included, that the feller weighed at least 500 pounds! It took us almost two hours to pack that critter out and Papa liked to have lost the horse and the wagon when that horse smelled the bear. We dressed the bear out there and I split some of the meat with Bill and Papa took some over to a feller in Hahira who made bear sausage out of a fair amount of it. We ate that bear through much of the winter. Mama tried a dozen ways to cook it but while it was okay, bear meat just didn't hold a candle to a nice venison steak or even a beef steak but as Papa said, you eat what you shoot and don't let anything go to waste.

Papa said he didn't want to see me going after any more bears in the future, especially with just buckshot and that was the only bear I ever shot. Truth be told, I'm not sorry. I like seeing them critters wandering around, especially if it was a Mama bear with cubs as they are the dangdest kind of critters for playing around and worrying their mama as any kind of baby animals I ever did see.

As I recall there was only a couple more times bears were spotted in our area and they must have just been passing through. I always felt kind of bad for this one as he'd hung around too long and had stirred up too much hunting blood in a youngster. I reckon that's the way life is sometimes. If a body happens to have a reputation for causing trouble, it's not a good idea to hang around too long. Someone bigger or badder—with more buckshot— might just happen along.

THE CHRISTMAS TREE

The first Christmas after I turned 12 I had an epiphany on how to get a Christmas tree earlier than normal. Papa had told me on my birthday that I was to be in charge of getting the next Christmas tree. Since I was born in the middle of October I had a little over six weeks to scout out a tree.

Now you have to understand…Christmas trees in south Georgia in those days were pretty much any decent looking pine tree that has the right sorta shape. We didn't have a bunch of folks selling Christmas trees in empty lots around town like they do today…trees specifically grown in Oregon or someplace out west to be cut and shipped all over to folks. Even if we had 'em, those trees are so artificial looking, my folks would have just laughed at em. They're so crowded with branches and needles it takes half an hour just to find a spot to hang an ornament.

No, our trees were local trees, usually just an old southern yellow pine but sometimes other vintages, like maybe a cedar. And they were always so spindly you could hang a draft horse sized ornament just about anywhere and still have room for its colt.

So, with the mission before me I started keeping an eye out for THE tree, in between my time in prison (aka, school) and hunting. It was rather a hindrance with regard to hunting because I was normally looking through the trees for a deer or maybe even a bear and just wasn't thinking about looking AT a tree. Now that I was obliged to find a tree, I discovered I was looking at the trees and twice missed seeing a buck until it was too late. I began to think the gift of picking out a tree wasn't all that great a gift.

Even so, I kept looking, for both the tree and of course, deer. About a week after Thanksgiving I found THE tree down near Elliot's Pond. Now Elliot's Pond was not exactly a pond as a body thinks of them. It was more of a wet open area in the middle of a bunch of oaks and a few pine trees scattered amongst them. A body had to be mindful walking out across it as it didn't have a solid bottom. Almost in the middle of the pond however was growing a small cedar tree perfectly shaped for our house and almost 8 feet tall.

"Perfect" I thought, that's just the tree. The only problem was hunting season was in full swing and I had heard other folks were scouring around looking for places to hunt as well as keeping their eyes open for Christmas trees and I was concerned that it would be gone before I got it. I knew it wouldn't be there in a couple weeks if I didn't get it quick, so I had to figure out how to cut that tree and keep it fresh until we could put it up the week before Christmas, as was our custom.

Well I pondered on that near all night 'fore I figured I could cut it down then drop it in the mill pond they used for keeping their cypress logs fresh. When the time came I could pull it out and it would be fresh and good to go into the parlor.

Using Bearl, our old draft horse, I dragged it on over to the millpond and dropped it in with no one the wiser. Only thing was, I hadn't considered just how heavy ol' Bearl was and I danged near got him stuck in that soft bottom before we got out of that pond area. I spent an hour giving him a good bath when I finally got him home.

Mama asked me every couple of days if I'd found a tree. I told her I had and it was a secret special tree and I had already harvested it. She was rather skeptical about that point, worrying it would be dead and the needles would have fallen off before we'd even put the candles and ornaments on it. I just told her it'd be as fresh as the day I got it and left it at that.

A few days later I started worrying about how the tree was doing and reckoned I'd better check on it. Yep, fresh as ever and I let it slip back into the water thinking myself pretty darned clever on things.

Finally the day arrived for us to dress up the house for Christmas. I went down to the pond and pulled the tree out in the morning and left it by the barn for a couple hours to drip dry. Along about noon, I dragged it on up to the house and Mama was pleased at how good the tree looked and how well I had done with my mission.

We dressed the tree up with all the candles and ornaments and put all the presents we'd made for each other underneath. In those days, we made something for somebody and didn't waste money on buying presents...as if any of us had any money to begin with. The most extravagant thing we did spend money on once in a while was wrapping paper and even that was rare.

That evening was December 20th and we'd had fried chicken, green beans (from Mama's canning earlier in the year) and squash for supper that night. As a special treat Mama had made us a peach pie from preserves she'd also canned up earlier that year. We all went into the parlor...if you call the one room with sitting furniture a parlor...to light the candles and sing some carols. We got the candles all lighted and were just picking out some songs from a songbook Papa had bought when we started hearing a kind of a tickling, swishy sound. No one could figure out what it was nor where it was coming from.

Our first song was Old King Wenceslas and we got through that and were working on Noel when I'll be danged if a dad-gummed little bass didn't drop on top of one of the presents. It was only a little feller about 3 inches long and before I could grab him, a whole slew of little fish started dropping down out of that tree. I reckon the heat from the candles caused 'em to start dropping all at once. My older sisters were laughing and the younger ones were screaming and running around the tree either trying to pick them up or shooing at them. Mama was laughing and Papa was hollering for us to grab 'em up and get 'em out of the house quick. All of us kids were grabbing up fish, from little minnows on up to a few semi decent sized breams all the while Papa was hollering about how the, you know what, fish got in the tree. After about an hour of doing our fishing, they seemed to be all cleared out of the tree. I left the bucket of dead fish out back of the barn for the cats to feast on and we all went to bed. Mama still smiling and Papa still grumbling.

Next morning I heard Papa growling again and got up to see what was wrong. Seems we hadn't got all those little fellers as there were still some laying under the tree and by now they'd started to give off a wondrous powerful fragrance that sure wasn't Channel Number Five. All the presents were removed as were the ornaments, and then the tree. I had to drag the tree out and put it back behind the barn, then go find another one. The second one wasn't near as nice as the first one but then it didn't provide as much aroma or amusement either...least ways not of the watery variety. Mama didn't fuss, just smiled. Even Papa chuckled once it was all done.

We had a grand Christmas that year and, of all things, I got a fishing rod from Papa. Orlee said I didn't even have to go outside to use it.

I never did anticipate that tree becoming a sanctuary for fish when I come up with my idea and I've taken a lot of ribbing over the years on that Christmas tree...not just from my parents but my "kind and sensitive" siblings have not only given me misery but they've made sure the story never stays hidden. I reckon I've been given close to 1000 danged fish ornaments over the years. Most are stuffed in boxes up in the attic now.

Now, if a body ever needs a bright idea for cutting a tree early and keeping it fresh, I can tell 'em how NOT to do it.

Merry Christmas to all you anglers out there.

BOYS, BIRDS, AND A HEN

The month before I turned 13 several of us conspired to head over to Miller Pond south of Ray City for a dove shoot. Miller Pond was at the short end of a millet field so we tended to call it Millet pond though I reckon old Mister Miller wouldn't have appreciated that. He had round about 40 acres planted with millet, cotton, corn, and sometimes a bit of tobacco. He, himself, wasn't a tobacco man so he didn't plant so much of that.

He reckoned corn and millet were cotton candy to a bird and the birds, doves in particular, laid waste to his millet fields every summer. He was happy to see the flocks thinned a bit and graciously accepted the generous portion of dove we left on his back stoop. He loved dove but he'd lost an eye years back and couldn't shoot birds real well though he purely knew how to put a permanent hurt on anything with fur and long legs.

We pretty much wandered through his fields with nary a complaint from him except for the time a couple of our sows got loose and ran crazy through his not quite ready to harvest cornfield with we boys hot in pursuit. My dog Stony added to the insanity, barking and dancing around.

So Mister Miller spoke to Papa and Papa gave us what for. Said if we'd just left 'em alone they'd have done a whole lot less damage before wandering home at their leisure. That was the last year we raised hogs so a repeat of that adventure never did occur and we never got to test out Papa's theory. It was probably just as well. Those hogs had grown as big as trees so I'd be rather concerned about a meeting now between them and Stony. Hogs are cute as the dickens when they're pups but come full grown they can hurt a body and I mean right now. I'd just as soon not see Stony trying to think he was some kind of hog dog.

Cat Creek prison (um...school) had opened up a couple weeks before and some of Mister Miller's harvest was still in the field so the three of us planned on heading over on Saturday around noon. The three including me was Frank Bottoms and Harley Winston. We all had farm chores to do so going early of a morning wasn't an option. Then Bo Henderson heard about it and wanted to make it four but he couldn't be there 'til one.

At lunch on Friday I told Harley and Frank about delaying the shoot and they were fine with that. While we were laying out our plans Emma June Smith walked by and kinda slowed her pace. I reckon she was listening to our plans but none of us paid any attention to Emma June. She was okay for a girl but we were doing man stuff and girl stuff just wasn't part of that conversation. Once she was out of earshot Harley asked if I thought she'd be a problem.

"What problem? She's a girl and girls can't shoot. And even if they could, we didn't invite her." Harley said he'd heard being invited and being there were two different things for Emma June and I just told him to go sit on a toad.

It was fairly cool the next morning, which was a welcome surprise. September in Georgia might be edging on towards fall but it was miles down the road from getting there. Hot and muggy was what we naturally expect right on up into October. Mel was still too young to go with us men so he moped around and told Mama things to try to get me in trouble and keep me from going.

We thought Mama didn't see everything going on around her and I still don't know what gave us that idea. She and Papa knew what we were thinking weeks before we even thought about them and when the time we were thinking about rolled around we'd be in trouble just fore thinking about doing any of those things. As it was, that morning Mama knew Mel was just being pestersome and told him he'd better rearrange his attitude fore she had a notion to rearrange his sitting ability.

Harley and Frank showed up right at noon and we set about loading up a small wagon, Mel's in fact, with the shotgun, shells, and sacks as well as some water and a few other emergency rations, like some boiled peanuts. Harley had even sweet talked his mother into giving us a loaf of fresh made bread. I grabbed a chunk of butter to go with it and those folks who think bread and butter and water alone ain't much ain't never had homemade bread and home-churned butter. That's certain sure. The only thing that could have made it better would have been if the bread was still warm but since Harley's mother had made it early that morning, it was close enough.

We were waiting for Bo to get to our place from Hahira when up the road we see someone coming. Harley grinned and said "I warned you".

I'll be danged. It was Emma June and she was tote'n a gun! She had on one of those store bought hunting vests I'd seen in a Sears and Roebuck catalog, too, and it was just bulging with shotgun shells. Her shotgun was kinda funny looking. I got to looking at it, sideways like of course, and realized what she had was a double barreled 410. Those little things hadn't been around very long so seeing one just made a body shake his head. They were tiny compared to the 12-gauge bruisers we were using.

We just kind o' laughed and teased her about it being a kid's gun. I asked her if she could hit anything with that toy. I was secretly impressed about the double barrel though 'cause I'd purely wanted one. But times being what they were, I'd made do well enough with my single shot 12.

Emma June didn't say anything in answer to my question 'cept "Reckon so". I fussed and fussed about having a girl, any girl, hunting with us men but it didn't seem to make no difference. Emma June just planted her feet and flat out said she was heading over to Miller Pond to shoot doves and we could join her or not. That had Frank and Harley laughing like fools and me highly annoyed but there wasn't any way around it.

Bo showed up a bit 'fore one and we headed on over to Miller Pond with Bo asking me who the girl was and was she my girlfriend and the other two jokers finding intense enjoyment at my chagrin and the chiding I was getting from Bo. Emma June also seemed to be finding humor in the fix I was in. Now, it wasn't that I didn't like girls but for me, it was an afternoon hunt with the boys. Having a girl along just weren't right.

After a while I got to thinking about that gun of hers and figured out how I could fix her wagon and make sure she wouldn't come out and crash our hunt again. When we got to the pond I told her we were all going to line up along some pine trees that ran down one side of the pond. I told her the birds typically flew in from the west between the pond and the trees. I said she could take the far end position and that anything we didn't get, she could try for with her little 410. She just looked at me and said, "That'll suit me. And I'll give half my birds to Mister Miller like you boys always do." That rankled but I looked at Bo and winked. Told her she could do that as an extra bird would surely be appreciated by Mister Miller.

So, that was it. We all got into position and loaded up. Bo was first in line, I was second, then Frank and Harley and finally Emma June. Now dove have pretty regular habits, pretty much like most critters, and once you know what those habits are you can position yourself to take advantage of 'em. One habit dove had was them flying down a couple hours towards dark in order to get a drink of water before going to roost for the night. Since the corn was still a week or so away from ripening that pretty much left the millet to attract the birds and they'd been keeping their eyes on it. They'd even tested a few of the older stalks and that's what prompted Mister Miller to call down to Papa and ask us to come over and thin 'em out.

We'd been sitting there pretty still for about half an hour when the first ones flew on in...early birds you could say. Well, they came in just a couple at a time like I saw those little fighter planes over in France a few years later. Bo hollered, jumped up, shot...and missed. I took my shot...and missed. Before that bird got much further Frank jumped up and winged it enough so as Harley could shoot it before it got to Emma June's area. "Well," I thought to myself, "not great, but she didn't get a chance." I was thinking this was going to work out just fine and we'd teach that hen about busting in on our shoot.

(Hens, I'd read in my Social Studies class, was what some o' them Australians called women. It sounded kinda disrespectful but I was feeling rather mean spirited at that moment. Truth be told, I was right put out about her being there. Later, when Mama found out about me using that term she gave me what for. I could call one a girl or a lady but they weren't chickens and if she heard me use that term again she'd put me right out in the coop with our birds. I saw no need to test her veracity.)

Next time, three birds came in together and I'll be danged if Bo and his 12-gauge double didn't miss them too! I hit one and it dropped like a rock but both Frank and Harley missed the remaining two. That's when we heard two little pops. Wasn't loud like a 12-gauge but softer and a bit sharper if that makes any sense. We all looked down the row and there was Emma June walking out to pick up two birds! Lord have mercy. She'd already made us look bad and it wasn't even heavy bird flying time yet.

Long about three thirty, or maybe a bit later, the wind picked up. That didn't help us none. Doves fly in a fashion that you have to admire even if you are trying to shoot 'em. They can twist and turn so fast you'd think they were always flying downhill. Add a bit of tailwind to the mix and your chances of hitting one of them feathered bullets go down pretty fast. And some of those birds must have figured out to come in a bit higher 'cause many of 'em were pushing the effective range of a 12-gauge, regardless of what kind of choke you had. The three of us had 12-gauges and Frank had a 16-gauge but they were all modified chokes. That means the pellets spread out a bit more than if they were full chokes which was for further out shooting. We found out the why of things at the end of the day.

Frank and Harley moved up towards the pond a bit but no matter what we tried that afternoon, it didn't seem to help a whole lot. Bo and I were trading about every fourth or fifth bird at best and every single bird that got by us got "popped" at the end and that durned hen was making us look like we were holding our guns backwards. We got so we started letting some go on through and would holler "EJ, here it comes"...and pop pop, the birds would drop. Emma June had her name reduced for effective hollering that day. Even poor old Stony was smiling I think. (It's always hard to tell whether your dog's laughing with you or at you but since he wasn't working particularly hard on panting, he sure looked like he was smiling.)

Long about six Mister Miller came out to see what kind of damage we'd done. We were all pretty much out of shells anyway as the birds were making us look silly and I figured we'd dropped enough lead on that field to weight it down an inch or two anyway. We gathered up our gear and walked on down to Emma June to divide up the spoils as we'd always done and that being the one thing I had insisted on with Emma June before we'd started.

I had 12 birds, Bo has 16, Frank 7, and Harley had 9. We figured that wasn't too bad considering how much the wind had picked up. The divvying up gave Mister Miller 20 birds to our 6 each. Emma June hadn't tossed her count in yet. I knew she had more than any one of us and was rather annoyed by that, but when she emptied her sack she had 36 birds ALONE! You just had to be there to see the look on Mister Miller's face.

This was the first time Mister Miller had met Emma June and he made the mistake of asking her if we'd loaded up her bag to make it look bigger. Before she'd said a word I caught a look that told me she was about to sound off. We didn't need to make Mister Miller mad for any reason so I said, "Mister Miller, we're all here to tell you we each shot what we shot and we kept our own birds. Seems that little 410 of hers just has a better choke on it than any of ours and it could reach out a bit further than we could but that's not the all of it. Emma June just plain outshot every one of us today and I ain't so sure I'd be keen to take her on in any sort o' competitive event. I'm here to tell you, Sir, you may be eating dove tonight but I think I'll be eating crow. I was a thinking it pretty humorous, them Australians calling girls hens but I'll tell you right now she's a killer and ain't no hen for sure. I'd like to see how she does on quail sometime and see if we could even out the playing field between these guns but I ain't ashamed to admit we got our hats handed to us today."

We loaded up all the birds into a pile and divided them all over again to make it fair for all. Emma June was calm and collected during all that and didn't complain about not being able to take home more of what she'd earned or about donating more than we did to Mister Miller. (He was all too happy to know he had plenty of good eating for the next few days.)

On the way back home I asked Emma June how she'd learned to be such a good shot. Seems her daddy was a fool for shooting clay pigeons, a hobby he'd picked up when they were in England for a couple of years. (To be honest, I'd clean forgot they'd been over there.) Anyway, Emma June had begun joining in on those shoots and she seemed to take to it, well, like a dove takes to flying. So he'd bought her that little double barrel and she showed, in the right hands, it wasn't nothing to be laughed at and boy, did she have the right hands.

To this day I've never looked at any gal wanting to hunt as being in any way a nuisance. I got humbled that day as did we all. Emma June went out with us a few times on the quail hunts and I got to be at least on par with her on them but then I'd been shooting at quail since before I'd even had a gun, that being with a slingshot.

She moved away a couple years after that and I never saw her again but I did read an article years later that she competed in some pretty fancy shooting events for a time. The day before she left she stopped me on the way out of church to say good bye. I'd never courted her, other than for hunting, and at that moment I wondered why. When had she turned from the smart-aleck hunting buddy to a nice-looking young lady? Quite nice in fact. I heard she'd married a fella out in Montana somewhere and they had some kind of ranch for raising buffalo. Well, she was some kind of woman.

I thought of Emma June when I started courting my wife, Ethylene. Try as I could, I couldn't interest her in learning to shoot or even going hunting with me, though I'll say she could sure turn a mess of birds into a fine meal. Ethylene said it was my job to collect the dinner fixin's and hers to cook 'em and that it didn't take two to do one or the other. It seemed a fair trade overall so I never complained about it. Ethylene was a grand gal and we raised a couple of great kids but I sometimes wished I could have talked her into sitting with me in a field just watching for doves.

PIGS AND HOGS
(DON'T YOU BELIEVE 'EM)

There were some folks who built a small house down on the south side of Cat Creek 'round about the time I was 10 or so. They were in kind of a swampy area where the land wasn't good for raising much besides water moccasins and mosquitos and I'm pretty sure even in those days there wasn't much call for either though I'm pretty sure most folks around would have been more than willing to sell either or both at an extremely reasonable price. But crops didn't grow well down there so they decided to raise pigs for market. They'd tried raising chickens but the 'coons, foxes, and 'possums pretty much cured 'em of that idea. The 'possums don't much bother a chicken but they get in and eat eggs if given half a chance. (Stony and I had a round or two over the years with those critters getting into our own chicken pens.) Given all that, pigs did seem a reasonable option.

Gertrude and Marvin Henley were their names. I disremember where they came from but they already had four little kids when they moved in, the oldest was about 7 or so. I don't recollect too much about the children as they were younger than any of us except Thelma. We were all pretty independent but she was still too young to go wandering all the way down to play at the Henley's farm just so's to bring back word of the goings on down there. It was 'most 4 miles from our place and that's a long way for walking but I was a mature 10 and found in the pigs the possibility of new and exciting adventures. This was several years afore we got our own taste of raising hogs.

Mister Henley wasn't what we considered particularly on the high rung of a ladder regarding education. He wasn't stupid mind you but Papa said he'd o' scored high if he was to reach the third rung. Mama shushed him about being critical as it wasn't a Christian thing to be thinking. Papa, she said, should be ashamed of himself for saying such things considering he didn't have much education himself.

This was true as far as book learning went but after looking back at what Papa could do and did with what little book-learnin' he had, you'd be forced to admit he'd moved on up past the first few rungs of that ladder, maybe even bein' in danger of going over the top step. I've known a lot of folks over the years that had a sight more education but they weren't any smarter than he was and a fair amount of 'em would have starved to death with what little they really did know about life and living in general. Some only managed to get into politics…a way of life which was, and maybe still is, considered a rather lowly profession and only fit for someone with long arms and short memories.

After the chicken farm disaster Mister Henley contacted some folks up in Nashville and arranged to pick up some young breeding pigs. I mean Nashville, Georgia not that other place. He went up in a hay wagon he'd rigged up with some small crates in it. Only thing was he hadn't reckoned on having to bring back a sow too. Seems the pigs weren't weaned yet and so the sow had to go along "on loan" until they were.

They had no way of loading that sow into the wagon even if she'd a' fit, so they loaded up the piglets in the crates and tied that sow on to the back of the wagon and walked her back. Mister Henley said you never heard such a racket in your life. Said them pigs squealed for mama the whole way back and that sow wasn't at all entertained at being tied on the back hearing her babies a squealing. She bit through the rope a few times before he finally managed to get 'em all home.

Now Nashville wasn't much over 15 miles away but in a wagon that's a mighty long way to go and it's even longer when you're pulling a hog back. It was dark by the time he got home so he just put the whole bunch into the pen and figured he'd sort 'em out in the morning. But when he got up the next day they'd disappeared. Understandably, Mister Henley was fit to be tied but he donned his boots, grabbed his shotgun and a couple heads of cabbage and set out on their trail. Caught up with them about a hundred yards from Cat Creek…only a quarter mile away. He didn't have much trouble drivin' 'em back to their pen. Said the sow actually turned out to be a big help that time. She must've cottoned on to him bein' the feller with the feed and since she had been pretty hungry it worked out well. Mister Henley just kept feeding her cabbage leaves as they walked back and of course the piglets just went where mama went. He sent Wilson Henley, the oldest boy, back to the house to get more cabbage 'cause that sow was worrying the two he'd brought along down to the core. Wilson showed up with a bucket of carrots and a couple onions and the sow must have been content to change up her diet a bit cause she kept right on following them all the way back to the house.

He spent the rest of the day rebuilding the pen and reinforcing it to keep all those critters in. But the little'uns found another escape route and that sow wasn't about to let her babies go wandering off without her so she just plain busted out a whole section of fence and followed along. We thought it fortunate they didn't run into any critters like a bobcat or a 'gator but, truth be told, that sow would have taken care of any moderately sized predator.

The next day, Mister Henley reckoned he'd left his sack of shotgun shells on a cypress stump when he'd been rounding up the sow so he went back to where he'd found the pigs. He found a spot down by the creek that was all torn up. He'd had other things on his mind when he was huntin' for the pigs so hadn't noticed it then. This time he walked around the spot and found 'bout half a water moccasin. Seems that mama didn't like snakes. Mister Henley checked the pigs when he got back but couldn't see any snake bites and they all acted fine so he assumed none had been bitten.

I've learned over the years that, while pigs ain't immune to snake poison, it takes a mighty big snake or a lucky strike (from the snakes perspective) to penetrate that hide. Besides that, pigs or hogs purely hate snakes and even the good kind is likely to be fodder for them. A few years later I saw one of our hogs get after a corn snake and that poor thing didn't stand a chance. It was half gone 'fore I could do anything to save it. We liked having the corn snakes around as they helped keep down the rats and mice around the farm but a hog just don't have the same kind of appreciation for the snakes as we did though they did their part in keeping the rodent population in check, too.

Mister Henley raised them piglets for close to a year before he started butchering and selling them. By that time they were most grown so mama hog didn't pay as much attention to them and she'd already allowed that humans were okay. Mister Henley had read a bunch of books and talked to other pig farmers during that year and learned how to cure and smoke the meat. He supplied the area with bacon and hams for several years. He'd turned out to be a pretty good pig farmer and did a right fine job on smoking and curing. Several years later he taught us how to smoke our own bacon and hams in appreciation for our help to his family.

After that first year I told Papa I reckoned Mister Henley was a bit higher than three rungs, which made Papa laugh and caused a few extra chores for me from Mama. They had close to 40 hogs all around the place and while everyone enjoyed the results, pigs are not exactly roses in a garden and there wasn't a thing you could do to get rid of the smell. The Henley kids were good kids but they ended up sitting on the edges of the classroom and hardly anyone would visit their farm as a result of the fragrant odors emanating from their folk's farm. Summers were both good and bad. Good 'cause we could get together and go swimming and that odor would mostly wash away. It was bad 'cause the cloud of pig fragrance seemed to waft farther out than during colder months.

The third year was the year that almost ended the pig farm. The mama sow had stayed on even after them first piglets were weaned 'cause Mister Henley had worked a deal and didn't have to take her back to Nashville. But that spring he lost her to a bear who'd woke from her winter slumbers with a powerful hunger. The younger hogs and pigs were pretty touchy after that. While they weren't what you'd call mean, they were pretty skittish and you had to be mindful to not let them get between you and the gate.

About a month after the bear attack Mister Henley went over to Ray City to deliver hams and such to a local grocer. Missus Henley went out to do the feeding and was in the pen scooting pigs around to scatter food out to where they all of them could reach it when a young sow took a swipe at her. A domestic hog doesn't have big tusks like some you see on a wild hog… tusks that'd scare Satan, but they do have tusks long enough to hurt a body.

That young sow caught Missus Henley's leg and sliced it open clear down to the bone. Andrew, the middle son, was with her and managed to get her out of the pen and back to the house. Those pigs went crazy when they smelled the blood and if Andrew hadn't been there, Missus Henley surely would not have got out alive. He got her to the house and the two younger Henley kids started screaming and hollering…all in a panic. Missus Henley was doing her best to reassure 'em she'd be all right though she was bleeding pretty bad. Wilson heard the ruckus and ran in from doin' his chores and wrapped her leg in a torn piece of sheet then he roped it down pretty tight to stop the bleeding. After that he sent Andrew over to us for help.

Papa had just come in from Hahira getting corn seed when Andrew came down the drive ahollerin' about his mama. Papa jumped back onto the wagon, corn sacks and all. Andrew and I barely managed to climb aboard 'fore he took off down the road to the Henley's house. Mama'd heard and made a call to Doctor Barrett down in Valdosta and he said it'd be best, if she was stable, to get her in to him as quickly as possible as he'd have a better chance of helping her if'n she was in the hospital. It didn't sound to him like it'd do much good for him to ride out to the Henley's. Papa made it to the Henley's house in about 20 minutes, pretty darned fast in a wagon. Missus Henley was still awake and still trying to get the children to calm down. Papa unwrapped her leg to change the bandage on account of all the blood then he and Wilson lost no time in boosting her up onto the corn sacks and headin' over to Valdosta to the hospital. Andrew and I took charge of the little'uns.

Doc Barrett sewed up the gash in her leg and ordered several transfusions of blood. She stayed in the hospital for nearly two weeks. She was left with a pretty impressive scar and she limped a bit for a year or so but that went away after a time. It was a miracle she didn't get an infection. We didn't have the antibiotics readily available they have nowadays. And speaking of times achangin', I only got to see the gash that one time and I never did see the scar the womenfolk talked about. In those days it was unseemly for a boy to see any part of a woman's leg, especially her thigh.

Before Papa and I arrived at the Henley's, Wilson went out and shot the sow. Might not a' been entirely the sow's fault but you can't blame Wilson for being angry and scared. When Mister Henley arrived at the farm late that afternoon he supported Wilson's action. Said there was a strong chance a sow would turn into a killer after a taste of blood.

While Missus Henley was in hospital he rebuilt all the hog pens so a body didn't have to go into the pen to feed and water. We used his pen plans when we got some hogs of our own. And by then we'd learned to never go near one without having something to drive 'em away from us.

Little pigs are cute but the older they get the more of that cute they lose. Some folks'll tell you hogs are smart and friendly. Only thing is, you have to be a lot smarter and a heap less friendly.

Mister Henley was grateful to us for helping the way we did and tried to give us a whole passel of hams and bacon. Mama refused his offer. Said we only did what Christian folks do. Said he could return the favor by helping someone else in need. And through the years he did just that. As I said earlier, he was not a well-educated man but he had a good Christian heart and he made it a point to help anyone in need. He even went into debt a couple times to do so and I reckon that's all the Good Lord can ask of a person... help your neighbor whoever he may be.

CORINNE AND HER GREAT MYSTERY

Martha Corinne is my oldest sister. Born in 18 and 88 she was seven years old when I come along. You may not think seven years would mean that much today or even then but it's still a long time between. Corinne was 17 when she married. It wasn't unusual for a girl of 17 to marry at that time and in fact, it was considered the norm. But Corinne, no one ever called her Martha as far as I ever heard, met a feller down in Valdosta who was a pharmacist and decided he was to be her beau. I don't remember much about that time but I do remember her telling Mama that she had met her mate and was determined to marry him. Mama didn't say much, as I recall. Seemed like she was almost relieved to have one less child to look after from what I could tell but remember, I was only 10. She did seem kind of sad for a bit and it wasn't until years later that I understood why.

Regardless, Corinne had set her sights on Fred and was determined to make her life with him. I thought it was a grand idea. I envisioned having one less person to share food and space with but I wasn't thinking about how things would change at home.

She'd met Fred coming home from church one Sunday morning. We were all going to the local Baptist church at the time, even though Mama said we were Methodists. But the nearest Methodist church was clear over in Hahira and that was almost 10 miles away. The Baptist church was only about 2 miles south of our farm and Mama said she was sure the Lord would understand that we were there to be praising Him and the longer we were in any church would be fine and that He would find us anyway. Course at the time I didn't have no idea about what the difference was between being a Methodist and Baptist but I do recall Papa talking to the Mister Jenkins one day about the difference. Papa said the main difference was that a Methodist could read. Mister Jenkins started laughing but I sure didn't understand at all, cause I knew Artemus and Nate Hanson who were Baptists and I know they could read...mostly.

Mister Jenkins owned the farm next to ours and like us, he raised cotton and corn and on occasion peanuts. He had two sons and three daughters. He'd had four sons but one was killed down in Cuba on some ship called the Maine as I recall. He sure was torn up about that for a long time but I was only three when it happened and only vaguely remember him coming over one evening and sitting with Mama and Papa talking in the kitchen. Franklin Wilkes Jenkins had only just turned 19 and I learned later had been down inside the ship. He'd only been in the Navy about four months. Mister Jenkins never really did get over that loss and I remember Mama saying that she never wanted to see any of us join the military. Said she'd heard enough about it from her folks. She reckoned wars should be fought by politicians and the innocent folks left out of it.

Humph, I guess I can wander off a storyline just about as well as my old dog Stony can wander off into the woods. Not too far off though...Frank Jenkins had been Corinne's love in '98 but she was 10 and he was 19, so it didn't figure to work too well.

After Corinne met Fred she couldn't wait to get to church and then she didn't want to come home. Then Fred moved to Valdosta where he'd been offered a job in a pharmacy. She spent two full days bawlin' about him and sayin' she didn't want to spend her life on a farm but wanted to live in a city. It took a good month before she started acting normal again. Course at the time I didn't know what normal was.

Girls were never considered normal when I was a kid and I ain't so sure about 'em now. But that wasn't my concern at the time. I was thinking about hunting and how soon I could get back out and scout for the old buck I'd been watching for about a month. Papa let me hunt birds with that 12-gauge but he hadn't yet approved of my owning a rifle. That meant I had to be pretty close to drop that old stag with buckshot.

It was January after our Christmas break and I was back in school. We knew we had four more torturous months before the prison, I mean the school, would release us. Corinne had worked hard to be able to graduate that year, a full year earlier than normal and we knew she would be going away. Papa had already promised to do what he could to help pay for college if that's what she wanted but he also said he couldn't see no good reason for a girl to go to college. But Corinne had made up her mind to go.

About the third week of January, we'd not been long to bed when we were woke up by barking dogs and squawking chickens. Papa grabbed his shotgun and ran out into the yard to shoot whoever or whatever it was that had decided to wake up the whole house, the chickens, the dogs, and probably the neighbors. Only thing was when he stopped in the middle of the yard there weren't nothing to be seen. I watched him from my window and he walked around the yard for a good ten minutes only to stop and scratch his head, yell at the dogs to shut up and then come back in the house. Mama was determined that some damned Yankee had tried to steal a chicken or two. At around midnight she finally made Papa go back out and count the chickens. Papa, not too keen on the idea, nonetheless agreed to go back out and count chickens. It wasn't a good thing overall, as he counted 'em and found that not only were they all there but that we had four new ones as well. I heard Papa making what I'll say was democratic comments on the state of chickens and had a word or two to say about dogs as well before he turned down all the lanterns and headed back to bed.

The next morning was a Sunday and we were all expected to be up, clean and ready to head to church as soon as breakfast was over. Only thing was, Corinne wasn't at the table yet. Mama was vexed, if I can say that, and told Oralee to go get her out of bed and tell her if she wasn't at table in 5 minutes, she'd just go to church hungry. Well, Oralee came right down and said Corinne wasn't in her room and said her bed was still made up but she had a note for Mama.

Handing the note to Mama, Oralee sat down to finish breakfast since ain't none of us ever figured there was truly a good reason to not eat or finish a breakfast. We thought that morning no different. Even though I was committed to eating as many of Mama's biscuits as possible, I noticed right off something was wrong. I saw Mama read that piece of paper and turn kinda white. She called for Papa, who happened to be just coming in from the barn. She told him to wash up and read that paper. Papa never was one to rush and I think it like to kill Mama for him to finally finish up and take that letter in hand. By then even my curiosity was up as I had finally stuffed down enough biscuits to slow me down a bit. I watched Papa read the letter then look at Mama. He slowly put it on the table and said, "Well, I reckon she's old enough to know better. I'll go into Valdosta in the morning and speak with Pastor Wilson at the church.

Now, you know, my papa wasn't one to just drop everything and take a day off. You had to take the day off if you were a going into Valdosta as, like I said it was almost 20 miles one way to get there so that pretty much took half a day each way.

Early the next morning, I woke to the sounds of horses and the jangling of the chains on the old wagon. The "courtin" buggy was a light two-seater and only needed one horse to pull it. It was also a lot faster so I had expected him to be taking that but Mama told us he was going to be in Valdosta for a couple of days and that the wagon would be needed to get some supplies.

Well I'll tell you, I was more than flummoxed. Papa never went to Valdosta for supplies lessen' he was in a dire need and as far as I knew, there wasn't anything he had to have right off. Still all Mama said was that he'd be gone at least a couple of days.

I'll be danged if the next day, a wagon showed up at the house with a feller from the Valdosta general store. He said he was out delivering some things and had got word to tell Missus Williams to gather her Sunday dress and head back to Valdosta with him.

Mama didn't argee; just told us she was leaving me in charge and she'd be switching the first child that got out of line while she was gone, including me. I promise you...she wasn't kidding.

So there we were, three boys and three girls and me in charge of the whole camp. I'd rather Papa had tanned my hide a half dozen times than to deal with that but the worst part was the not knowing. What was going on? Why had Papa gone? Why had he sent for Mama? Where was Corinne? We got through it somehow and on the third day both Mama and Papa came riding in on our old wagon and with a bunch of supplies Papa thought we might be needin'. Not needed mind you, more like "kind" of needed. Papa didn't say a thing about his trip but just told me to unhitch the wagon, put the supplies away and tend to the horses then come into the parlor.

I did all that, all the while just bustin' to know what was going on. I was almost 11 at that time and I figured I was danged near a man. It wasn't til much later I learned that being a man was about more'n just age. At 11, I was just beginning to think about it but not until 8 years later did I learn what it really meant.

After I'd finished the chores Papa called the rest of us into the parlor and said he had some bad news and some good news to tell us. He was quiet for a bit then finally seemed to sort out what he wanted to say. "Quiet", he bellowed. Well that wasn't anything as we'd all been quiet as church mice.

"I want to tell you kids that your sister Corinne has done got herself married off to a feller in Valdosta. He seems to be a fine fellow and he's a pharmacist. That's a feller who gives out medicine a doctor prescribes. I ain't sure what all he can do besides that and also run a soda fountain but it seems to me, she done hitched herself to a new life."

That being said, he added that he thought the feller was a pretty decent soul and had met with him a couple of times and then they all went before a judge who said he agreed they could get married and that was pretty much it. Mama fussed that she wanted to give Corinne a church wedding and have all the folks in but Papa said he was content that she was married in front of an official judge and that was fine and proper as far as he was concerned.

So Corinne's mystery was only a secret marriage, much less of a mystery than us children had been thinking for 3 days...though it seemed like weeks and weeks. We figured she'd run off with a sideshow in a circus and were sore disappointed to find out it was just her getting married by a judge. Joining a circus would have been much more interesting.

As for Mama, I don't think she ever thought the marriage a proper one but she didn't have no say in it and as it turned out I don't think it mattered. Corinne and Fred had seven children and most all of them went off to college. I think most of the boys went to pharmaceutical college somewhere and followed in their daddy's business. I recollect only one of the girls did.

Fred and one of his brothers became Freemasons a few years latter. At the time, no one else in the family had ever been a Freemason. Not because we considered ourselves poor folk but being a member of that society was something that required a bit of money not earmarked for some necessity or another. I heard Papa saying one time that he thought about joining but that the cost was just too much and he figgerd he'd have to be content with donating what he could to the church instead, which in the end was probably mor'n what it cost to join but I reckon Papa wasn't a joining kind of person anyway. He figured there was too much to do with the farm and family to be taking time out for that kind of socializing. Myself, I never did join. Like Papa, I had too many other things going on to do so. Don't get me wrong, I think they're a fine group of fellows but I just never had the extra time to give them.

I suspect the elopement of my sister Corinne was the beginning of my lifelong suspicion of females. Ain't trusted 'em since then and I've done been married for 45 years now.

CPSIA information can be obtained
at www.ICGtesting.com
Printed in the USA
JSHW052003151122
33258JS00002B/7

9 781734 143737